# DANIEL

## John G. Gammie

---

# KNOX PREACHING GUIDES
## John H. Hayes, Editor

## John Knox Press
### ATLANTA

With gratitude to
Helen, John, Stephen, and Alison
for what they have been teaching their parents
from even before they went to study
a foreign language and literature
in distant courts

**Library of Congress Cataloging in Publication Data**

Gammie, John G.
    Daniel.

    (Knox preaching guides)
    Bibliography: p.
    1. Bible. O.T. Daniel—Commentaries. 2. Bible. O.T.
Daniel—Homiletical use. I. Title. II. Series.
BS1555.3.G35    1983    244'.507    83-6803
ISBN 0-8042-3224-5

© copyright John Knox Press 1983
10 9 8 7 6 5 4 3 2 1
Printed in the United States of America
John Knox Press
Atlanta, Georgia 30365

# Contents

# DANIEL

## Introduction

The book of Daniel follows Ezekiel in the English Bible and thus is frequently, but not quite accurately, classified with the prophets. In the Hebrew Bible Daniel occurs in the third, and last, section called the Writings. For this and other reasons (chiefly loan words and the historical surveys in chapters 2, 7, 8 and 11), Daniel is regarded by most modern scholars as coming from the time of the Maccabees (about 164 BC) rather than from the time of the Babylonian Exile (586–538 BC). This late dating does not affect the book's magnificent teaching on the faithfulness of God, the power of God to raise up and depose kings, the coming of a heavenly kingdom, and the limits God usually places upon the operation of blasphemous rulers.

Daniel was recognized to be the name of a well-known ancient worthy whose righteousness was on a par with that of Noah and Job (Ezek 14:14). It is less widely recognized that Daniel was also the name of the second son of David (1 Chron 3:1), hence a royal name, as well as a priestly name in the family of Ithamar (Ezra 8:2). The name Daniel means: "God is my Judge" or, more accurately, "God is the Defender of my Right."

Half of the book (chapters 2—7) is written in Aramaic, a sister language to Hebrew. Scholars have not yet come up with an altogether convincing explanation for the two-fold languages in the book—except that perhaps these chapters especially were meant for the pagan overlords to hear, because Aramaic was a language of international exchange (*lingua franca*) during the Babylonian, Persian and Greek periods.

The book may be outlined as follows:
Daniel 1—6: Stories on God's reward of faithfulness (or punishment for its absence!).
Daniel 7—12: Visions of the Future.

In chapters 1, 3 and 6 Daniel and/or his three companions are confronted with tests of their faithfulness. Even at the risk of death (chapters 3 and 6), they choose to remain true to their God. The message of these chapters is this: God is loyal to those who show themselves loyal (see Psalm 18:25–29).

Chapters 4 and 5 present portraits of a monarch—two sides of a coin: one learns humility in the course of his mental illness and has the kingdom restored to him (chapter 4); the other, who is blasphemous and arrogant, is less fortunate (chapter 5). We are reminded of the parable of the fool told by Jesus (Luke 12:16–21).

Chapters 2 and 7 are companion chapters portraying the succession of world empires which will be succeeded by a fifth which will be presided over by "the Coming One, like a Son of Man." Much ink has been spilled in identifying the successive empires, and the defiant "Little Horn" in 7:8, 20–21. Interpretations range widely—the Pope, Napoleon, Hitler, and even more recent characters! These attempts to "update" were, and are, examples of ingenious (and sometimes, sad) eisegesis, that is, reading of an erroneous meaning into the text. The original author had his own specific candidate whom scholars are able to identify with reasonable certainty as the Greco-Syrian king, Antiochus IV Epiphanes (175–163 BC).

History is told in this book in symbolic terms (chapters 2, 7, 8 and 11). For the most probably correct interpretation and identification of the characters in these chapters, see the commentary below. In chapter eight, there is no debate on the issue of identification because the text is explicit. The chapter describes the victory of "the he-goat" over "the ram with the two horns." "The two horns" are explicitly identified as "the kings of Media and Persia" (v. 20). "The conspicuous horn" on "the he-goat" (v. 5), who is also called "the great horn" (v. 21), is also explicitly identified as "the king of Greece . . . the first king" (v. 21), that is, as virtually all scholars agree, Alexander the Great. Because the chapter is so explicit, the majority of scholars maintain that this chapter (and chapters 2, 7 and 11 as well) comes not from the period of the Exile, but from the period after Alexander the Great. Conservative scholars view these chapters of historical survey as predictions; a more defensible understanding of them is that the author is simply employing a regular convention of apocalyptic literature—writing history in the form of prediction.

The author is certainly concerned with biblical and other predictions. The meaning of Jeremiah's prophecy of a 70 week exile fascinates him (9:1–2, 20–27), as does the length of the period of cessation of the continual burnt offerings and how the "king" will come to his end (11:40–45).

The successive attempts for the author to stipulate how long it will be before these offerings are restored (8:13–14; 9:27; 12:11–13) serve to demonstrate that even the sacred writers ran into difficulties when they sought to place definite timetables on the end point of their woes. Jesus mildly chided against such speculations (Mark 13:33).

The preacher should be sure not to overlook Daniel's magnificent prayer in 9:3–19 nor to miss Daniel's encounter with heavenly emissaries (chapter 10) or the book's stirring words on the resurrection (12:1–4).

At least two stages in the development of the book may be readily observed from even the most casual reading. On the one hand, there is a qualified openness to the culture of the pagan overlord (chapter 1). Daniel and his companions are sent to the foreign court to learn the language and literature of their foreign captors. Even though some of the foreign bureaucrats may be presented at this stage as malicious and scheming (chapters 3, 6), not all of them are so presented (the steward in chapter 1 is sympathetic and cooperative) and frequently the foreign king is depicted in a friendly light: he looks on Daniel and his companions favorably (1:20; 5:14) and rewards them (2:48–49; 3:30) and praises their God (2:47; 4:1–3; 4:34–35; 6:26–27). This, probably earlier, stage in the book's development hardly comes from a period of deep hostility to, or rejection of, the pagan overlords. On the other hand, some of the passages in the book show a marked shift in attitude toward the foreign king: in chapter 5 he desecrates the sacred vessels taken from the temple in Jerusalem; in chapter 7 foreign rule is portrayed as beasts—instead of as metals, as in chapter 2; and one horn, a "little horn" (8:9), makes war with the saints (7:21), desecrates the temple, and cuts off the continual burnt offerings (8:9–13). The second stage clearly comes from the time of the Greco-Syrian (Seleucid) ruler, Antiochus IV whose anti-Jewish policies are fully chronicled in the books of 1 and 2 Maccabees; whereas the earlier portions of the book come from the period of the Ptolemaic predecessors perhaps, as seems to me likely, from the time of Ptolemy IV (221–203 BC) who was friendly to the Jewish communities in Egypt and Palestine at first but then became increasingly hostile and erratic. (For an exaggerated description of this ruler, see the book of 4 Maccabees.) Scholars may differ on details but the agreement is widespread that most, if not all, of the stories of Dan 1—6 come from *before* the period of revolt against Antiochus IV under Judas Maccabeus and that the visions of Dan 7—12 are largely from the time of the Maccabean Revolt and afterwards.

On the third, deutero-canonical and Greek, stage in the book of Daniel, see our opening comments below on chapter 12. Translations of these so-called additions to Daniel may be readily found in any edition of the Protestant Apocrypha or a Catholic edition of the Old Testament.

## The Hazards of Preaching From Daniel

Preaching from Daniel can be an exciting and rewarding endeavor. It also has its hazards, and the present preaching guide has been designed to help the pastor to think through how he/she may enhance his/her enjoyment in preaching from the book and at the same time strengthen the faithful. The excitement of preaching from Daniel derives precisely in part because it is not without hazards.

Some of the important questions confronting the preacher in the book are discussed below in the introductory sections to chapters 3, 7 and 8. Should the pastor tell the congregation in any one sermon all he/she knows about the apocalyptic literature? (Probably not.) Are those persons all wrong who think we can see in Daniel accurate forecasting of contemporary, modern events? (Probably not?) Even though there may be differences in interpretation of the book among persons from all parts of the theological spectrum, are there profound theological assertions in the book which theists, including Christians of all stripes, may wholeheartedly affirm? (Certainly yes.) In the following chapters of this book I have supplied a number of mostly three-point sermon outlines. All of them grew out of, or were triggered by, the text of Daniel. Indeed, some of my comments on the text of Daniel are to be found in the outlines. Other suggested sermon outlines seek not only to identify but also to show the way of addressing directly some urgent issues raised by the book on miracles, prayer, true patriotism, mental health, modern idolatries, the crystal ball approach to the Bible, Christian indebtedness to the Jewish community, patterns in history, the meaning of the Kingdom of God, resurrection, and others. As Fred Craddock has so eloquently reminded us (*As One Without Authority* and *Overhearing the Gospel*), all sermons should not be three-point sermons! Some variety in the pulpit is necessary for effective communication. The book of Daniel itself is an example. It shifts from marvelous stories in the first part to grand visions in the second part. There is great drama and mounting tension in the stories. There is colorful imagery and keen historic awareness in the visions.

Because angels are a recurring feature in Daniel, some suggestions have been included below under chapters 4 and 12 on how the preacher might approach this topic. An angel mentioned elsewhere in the Scriptures also furnishes an important clue as to how this book and others of the Knox Preaching Guides might best be used. In Gen 32:22–32 Jacob wrestles long and hard with a mysterious man before the latter blesses him. The text itself doesn't call the "man" an angel but we do. No matter. A sermon that blesses must be wrestled with beforehand with tenacity, prayer, and determination. It is my hope that this Guide and its sermon outlines will be for you as an angelic sparring partner.

### Understanding Apocalyptic

The book of Daniel belongs, with the book of Revelation (Greek: *apokalypsis*) in the New Testament and the book of

2 Esdras in the Apocrypha, to that class of literature called apocalyptic. Books which resemble Daniel, Revelation, and 2 Esdras may be classified as apocalyptic. The name apocalyptic is derived from the Greek *apokalypsis* which means "unveiling, uncovering, or revelation." The works in this category thus always contain some unveiling or uncovering: of secrets on earth, or of events transpiring in the heavens, or in the future, which are hidden from ordinary human eyes. In the book of Daniel such unveilings occur in chapters 2, 4, 5 and 7—12. They are frequent, of course, also in the Apocalypse (the book of Revelation).

Apocalyptic literature is a complex or composite class which may be identified by whether or not there is present in any given work a cluster of sub-types or component forms which regularly recur in the class, such as: vision reports of events in the heavens or in the future; historical surveys told with colorful, and frequently animal, symbols as if they were visions of the future; dialogue with angels; hymnic and liturgical praises to God; dream reports; riddles and interpretations of riddles; interpretations of dreams; and interpretations of visions. The apocalyptic literature, which flourished in the period 200 BC to AD 100, also contains a cluster of regularly recurring ideational elements (ideas) such as: resurrection; belief in the correspondence of heavenly happenings and earthly events; a coming judgment; exhortation to faithfulness; and descriptions of events which will lead up to the end of days. (The latter are called in the rabbinic literature, "the footprints of the Messiah.") In the New Testament, Mark 13, Matt 24 and Luke 21:5–36 are frequently classified as apocalyptic or "little apocalypses" precisely because scholars recognize in them the requisite clusters of ideas and of sub-genres typical of apocalyptic. Up until recently the term apocalyptic was understood to mean almost exclusively a bizarre and strange imagery pertaining to the end of days (eschatology).

Modern study of apocalyptic in the English-speaking world, not altogether accidentally, has witnessed major advances during, or just preceding, times of war. If scholarly interest in apocalyptic is an accurate weathervane of tumultuous times and of man's inability to control the beast of violence and war within and anarchy and despotism without, then the present and future do not look very hopeful, for the past two decades have witnessed an unremittant outpouring of books and articles on biblical and extra-biblical apocalyptic writings and themes.

One of the major advances in understanding apocalyptic has been the identification of parts of the Bible outside of Daniel and Revelation which belong either to this same class or have many affinities with it. Modern study has shown that the apocalyptic literature did not drop suddenly on the scene as a fully developed form of literature. The way has rather been prepared in parts of the prophetic books such as Ezek 1—3; 16—17; 21; 34; 38—39; 47; Isa 24—27; Joel; Zech 9—14; and even Zech 1—8. In the New Testament, scholars point to the common source of Matthew and Luke (Q) and to First and Second Thessalonians as further examples of works and writings with a heavy apocalyptic influence. Ernst Käsemann, professor of New Testament at Tübingen, Germany, went so far as to say that "apocalyptic was the mother of Christian theology."

Modern study of apocalyptic has also stressed the importance of the many extra-biblical apocalyptic or apocalyptic-like works which have come under increasing scrutiny in recent decades. At the head of the list is clearly 1 Enoch—a Jewish work once thought to come from the second century BC, but now, since the discovery of Aramaic fragments of this book among the Dead Sea scrolls, argued by some scholars to antedate in part the book of Daniel. In this book, the reader is taken on a heavenly journey with the ancient dignitary Enoch (on whom see Gen 5:21-24) who is asked to intercede for fallen angels, who sees a heaven of blissful reward for the righteous and places either hard and rocky, or fiery, for punishment for the wicked. In a section of this book apparently later than the Dead Sea scrolls, reference is made to the "Son of Man," a semi-divine figure who will bring humankind into judgment.

Two other works with apocalyptic elements which throw light on the book of Daniel should also be mentioned. The book of Tobit is a delightful story of the triumph of good. (Hebrew *tob* means good.) It is readily available in the Apocrypha or a Catholic Bible and is a treasure trove of material for sermon illustrations because of its high melodrama. The adventures of Tobias, son of Tobit, purportedly transpire, as do the stories and visions of Daniel, during a time of Exile—in this instance, the Assyrian Exile that took place following the fall of Samaria. In the same way that angels assume a role of prominence in the book of Daniel, in Tobit the angel Raphael ("Healer of God") travels in the guise of a human servant, to protect Tobias on his journeys from, among other things, a man-eating fish and from a death-bearing demon by the name of Asmodeus. The work contains a beautiful prayer of praise (chapter 13) similar to the doxologies in Daniel and, incidentally, a marvelous story (chapters 6—8) and prayers 8:5–7, 15–17) suitable for re-telling or use even today at weddings.

The *Testaments of the Twelve Patriarchs*, like Tobit and Daniel, holds up its heroes as models of virtue and conduct to be emulated. Like Tobit, it was composed around 200 BC. In the testament bearing his name, Joseph especially is extolled as a worthy example of non-vengeful, self-giving love. This work is not yet too accessible but if you are on a study leave it is well worth digging out in James H. Charlesworth (ed.), *The Old Testament Pseudepigrapha*. After reading it, I first became aware of how many parallels there are between the careers of Jesus and Joseph (Genesis 37—50). Some interesting sermonic comparisons might be made between Joseph and Daniel, Daniel and Jesus, and Jesus and Joseph. For some specific ideas for developing these associations, see the comments below on chapter six. Like the books of Daniel and Tobit, the *Testaments of the Twelve Patriarchs* also contains material especially suitable for sermons directed to youth; for example, Simeon is held up as a negative prototype of jealousy and envy; Gad of hatred and anger; Dan of lying; and Reuben of unchastity. Positive prototypes are Judah (of courage and temperance), Naphtali (of kindness and purity), Zebulun (of compassion and mercy) and Joseph (of chastity and humility as well as of love). R. H. Charles rightly extolled the high level of moral teaching in this book. Its teachings on the spirits of demons tempting youth are phrased with an admirable blend of humor and sound morality which would lighten up and make effective any sermon touching on sexuality, use of alcohol, and self-control.

**The Pattern of the Stories: Fidelity Rewarded**

The first six chapters of Daniel are self-contained stories, each masterfully told with a moral for Judean youths *and* secular overlords. Recent studies in structuralism, folklore, story, and the ancient romances may help us to be more sensitive to the inner dynamics of these stories. Just as Vladimir Propp has shown how in the Russian folktale a limited number of functions of characters are to be found in them (and in the same sequence), so in the ancient romances, as in Dan 1—6, a limited number of fundamental elements in sequence may be observed.

BASIC EPISODES (FUNCTIONAL ELEMENTS)

(1) Decision, dilemma, or decree of the king which threatens (or challenges) the life-style or life of the faithful Judean(s).

(2) Resolve of the faithful to remain loyal to the Most High God and/or to turn to him for aid.

(3) A period of trial or testing, followed by:

(4) A successful outcome, and

(5) A decision or decree of the king, in favor of the Judean(s) and/or their God.

Sometimes the first episode is introduced by villainous fellow courtiers who, out of jealousy, induce the king to pass a threatening decree (chapter 6) or who maliciously accuse the Judeans of non-compliance (chapter 3). Each one of the chapters, however, contains the above functional elements in the sequence given.

The stories of Dan 1—6 may also be labelled "apologues." They defend the correctness of fidelity to the Most High God through showing that, in most instances, both the faithful youth and secular overlord will benefit through such fidelity. Touches of satire may be observed in each one of the stories.

In common with ancient romances, the tales of the book of Daniel demonstrate that the deity will both care for and protect loyal devotees. At least one sermon based on Daniel 1—6 might be devoted to the main theme of the stories: God rewards faithfulness. The sermon outline might well follow the sequence listed above. If the outcome seems too pat, too slick, the preacher might choose to follow the sermon on Dan 1—6 with one on the book of Job!

# The Quiet Working of God
## (Daniel 1:1–21)

Even though the indications are fairly plain that this chapter comes from an earlier stage in the development of the book (on which see above), the chapter serves as a suitable introduction to the entire work. It introduces Daniel and his friends to the Chaldean court and court officials, records the capture of the sacred vessels from the temple in Jerusalem (the desecration of which features in chapter 5), and sets forth a paradigmatic storyline which is repeated in the five subsequent chapters. Through placing the stories in the context of the Babylonian Exile, the author is plainly speaking to an audience wherein the problem of living under later pagan overlords could be given full play.

There is a subtle, but unmistakably satiric, dimension to the chapter. The butt of the satire is the bureaucratic chain of command. The chapter moves from the king to the chief eunuch to the guardian (vv. 3–10)—and then, on back through the chain of command (vv. 11–16). The name of the chief eunuch, Ashpenaz, contains the root for the Hebrew word "sorcerer" and may itself be a gentle spoof because it means in translation "Sprinkling Sorcerer." In the Septuagint Ashpenaz is named instead Abiesdri which means (in Hebrew) "Father of my Order." The author seems to take delight in the Hebrew overtones of the names given to Daniel and his friends.

NAMES OF THE FOUR YOUTHS IN DANIEL

| Original Hebrew Name | Meaning | Newly Bestowed Chaldean Name | Meaning (in Hebrew) |
|---|---|---|---|
| Daniel | "My God Judges" or "God is the Defender of my Right" | Belteshazzar | "He bears Adversity in secret" |
| Hananiah | "Yah is Gracious" | Shadrach | "He who follows the Way" |
| Mishael | "Who is what God is?" | Meshach | "Abating Waters" |
| Azariah | "Yah helps" | Abednego | "Servant of Affliction" |

The Chaldean names appear to be as carefully chosen for their theological import as were the Hebraic names. It is a common device in literature—the biblical literature included—to select (or stress how) the names of characters epitomize or foreshadow the character or fate of the name-bearer, e.g.: Abraham ("Father of many people"), Jacob ("He supplants"), Israel ("He who strives with God"); Richard Diver in Scott Fitzgerald's *Tender is the Night*; Steerforth in Charles Dickens's *David Copperfield;* the Reverend Arthur Dimmesdale in Nathaniel Hawthorne's *Scarlet Letter;* and Phyllis Thanatophilos ("Deathlover") in Evelyn Waugh's hilarious and macabre *The Loved Ones.* In Daniel, the new name given to Mishael already contains an anticipation that the time of trial has a foreseeable terminus: the waters will abate. The new names given to Daniel, Hananiah, and Azariah which on the surface are Chaldean names, contain a clear affirmation for the Hebrew reader of the character of the youth who bears the name.

## Education/Strategies in Relation to Culture (1:1-4)

The opening verses of Dan 1 focus on a great challenge beyond tragedy. The tragedy: the city of Jerusalem is besieged (v. 1) and her king delivered by God into the hands of the conqueror (v. 2). "And the Lord gave Jehoiakim . . . into his hand." The primary agent in history is God. Human suffering, the anguish and heartache attendant upon this tragic event so apparent in Jeremiah and in the book of Lamentations, is not the focus of attention, but rather the conquering king's call for qualified Jewish youths to be educated in the Chaldean language and literature (vv. 3-4). Two different sermons could be developed from these verses on (1) the importance and limits of education and (2) alternative attitudes which religious/Christian communities may take toward secular culture. A sermon on "The Cost and Challenge of An Education" might be developed along the following lines.

(A) The requirements and cost of a secular education may not always be easy to calculate in advance. (1) There may be pain because not everyone is selected. Those chosen were to be "of the nobility," "without blemish," "skillful," etc. Not everyone belongs to the nobility: the selection pro-

cess is painful for those eliminated. (2) The hidden and unan-
ticipated costs may be high. Was it understood that those
selected would have to become eunuchs? The chief eunuch
issued the call for applicants (v. 3). The early church fathers
were deeply troubled by the implications that the subservi-
ence of Daniel and his companions to the chief eunuch (v.
8) meant that the price they had to pay for their education was
to be rendered eunuchs themselves! Eunuchs were individuals who through little or no say on their part were unable to
enter into normal sexual relations. The testicles were either
crushed or the male member cut off (Deut 23:1). A costly education indeed! Interestingly, the rabbis (in contrast to the
church fathers) accepted that this was the price Daniel and
his companions had to pay.

(B) Education is of importance on at least three counts.
(1) *For one's own self.* The verses contain no panegyric on the
advantages of learning the letters and language of the
Chaldeans—they presuppose it. According to the teaching of
Aristotle, the road to happiness lies in the use and development of natural endowments. In the Judeo-Christian tradition the love of God with the mind—and development and
use of that mind in the service of God—is a major way to self-
fulfillment and wholeness. (2) *For one's own people.* Trained
bureaucrats would be in a position to aid and to keep an eye
out for the needs of the group or sub-culture from whence
they came. Education furnishes the opportunity to serve
one's own. (3) *For inter-group relations.* David Riesman and
Christopher Jencks point out in a book called *The Academic
Revolution* that the diploma (lit. "twice-folded [document]")
was carried by ambassadors from ancient Greece to other
countries. The holders of diplomas today are ambassadors,
spokespersons, between sub-cultures. In a pluralistic society
such as ours, without such ambassadors functioning, our society would fly apart.

(C) The limits of education should nonetheless be acknowledged. (1) Knowledge is not a cure-all. Knowledge,
even knowledge in technology or about moral systems, is not
a panacea for the world's ills. Scientism, an inflated confidence in the ability of knowledge (*scientia*) to procure for humankind a brighter future, is as much a quasi-religion as
nationalism—and as idolatrous. (2) The need for spiritual

maturity remains. Control of technology, and of the beast
(greed) within, requires not only superior knowledge and
self-awareness but leaders with a clear sense of human
pretensions and human capacity for self-deception and ava-
rice. (See esp. Dan 4.) Idolatries in the end are self-defeating—even the idolization of knowledge. Faith, profound
belief in the divine governance, is a necessary requisite for
the ultimate advancement of every sub-culture and culture.
(For further thoughts on idolatries and the divine sovereignty, see the comments below on chapters 3 and 4.)

Related to the above sermon would be the following:
"Alternative Strategies in Relation to Secular Culture." Major points to be treated might be the following.

(A) Some religious groups have taken a stance opposite
that of Dan 1:1–4 (Christ is against Culture). (1) This stance
of separation and withdrawal and radical rejection of the
culture of secular or pagan overlords is found in the book of
Revelation, 1 John, Tertullian, monasticism, Protestant sec-
tarianism and Leo Tolstoy. (2) This stance accentuates the
seductive, corrupting aspects of culture, tending to limit the
realms in which the grace of God is operative to the specifi-
cally religious. (3) This stance in the end either (a) designates
a number of areas of life where the divine is only marginally
operative, if at all, or (b) it fosters a dualistic world view
which sees human existence basically as a battleground between forces of good (God) and of evil (Satan).

(B) Some religious groups have taken a stance even more
accommodating to culture than Dan 1:1–4 (Christ is of Culture). (1) This stance of nearly unquestioning accommoda-
tion to secular culture is found in Christian gnostics, Peter
Abelard, the so-called "Culture-Protestantism" of Friedrich
Schleiermacher and Albrecht Ritschl and in the so-called
Christian liberalism. (2) This stance sees God operative in
virtually all areas of life but fails to distinguish between
Christianity and middle class values. The so-called "Moral
Majority" rightly places "humanistic liberalism" in this category but fails to see how its own uncritical militaristic nationalism partakes of the same idolatrous aspects it descries.
(3) The humanistic aspect of this stance is deeply biblical:
that God turns toward needful humankind is the burden of
both Testaments. For all of its faults, this stance does not put

limits on the areas into which the divine Spirit can reach. It fosters an activistic and compassionate involvement of believers in human affairs.

(C) Some religious groups follow the pattern of involvement of Dan 1:1–4 (Christ is the Transformer of Culture). (1) This stance, which sees the religious community as called to be agents of the conversion of culture, is found in Dan 1—6, Isa 40—55, the Gospel of John, St. Augustine, St. Thomas Aquinas, John Calvin, and John Wesley. (2) This stance does not advocate withdrawal from culture but participation in it, confrontation and conversion. It is grounded not in a narcissistic desire to preserve personal purity by self-isolation but rather in a hope which affirms the forgiveness of sins and places ultimate confidence in God to transform and regenerate. (For further ideas, nuances and variations on this second sermon suggestion, the reader may consult with profit H. Richard Niebuhr's *Christ and Culture*.)

## College/On Being Alone/Beyond the Boundaries (1:5–8)

These verses bring to a head the challenge and response of pursuit of an education in a pagan court: (i) it is expected that all applicants will conform to the local patterns of food and drink (v. 5); (ii) even distinctive Judean names are discarded to facilitate acculturation (vv. 6–7); but (iii) the young Daniel resolves not to abandon the Judean dietary laws (v. 8). Three sermons may be developed from these verses. The first might be called, "So You're Going to College," and might consider the following points.

(A) *The challenge and opportunities of an education.* This section could be similar to section B in the first sermon suggested above, or, it could focus on such things as: (i) the importance of developing the imagination, (ii) the difference between mere acquisition of skills and the development of one's ability to analyze critically, and (iii) the role of literature and the humanities in expanding one's sensitivity to the complex interplay of social, psychological, and aesthetic factors in shaping human conduct.

(B) *The trial for the student* (using direct address). (1) Not only your own individual character and moral fibre will be put to the test but also the value-systems of your high school peers, your church, and your parents. (2) As important as how you (the student) respond to new challenges and temptations will be how we at home respond. Will we (the parents, teachers, and church leaders) be open to criticisms you may bring on the value-systems we outwardly (and inwardly) affirm? Will we be open to see where we have been hypocritical? Will we be open to growth?

(C) "*But Daniel Resolved.*" (1) There will be problems arising from loneliness, peer group pressure, removal of parental restraints. (2) Acquisition of knowledge and development of character depend on a degree of resolution, self-discipline. (3) Parents and church share in the excitement of the new challenge, with confidence, support of thoughts and prayers, and hope.

Another sermon, not directed to the nuclear family, but to a much neglected group, single persons: bachelors, spinsters, widows, widowers. (See also Jer 16:1–4.) You could call the sermon, "On Being Alone." The development of this sermon might take the following tack.

(A) To begin to know one's own and others' personhood, we may start with our names and nicknames (and their meaning) and how to deal with aloneness. (1) This section could start with: "Among these were Daniel, Hananiah, Mishael, Azariah" and an explanation of the meaning of these names (see above) and other (including some women's) names. (Most dictionaries provide lists of names and their meanings.) (2) Individual names and nicknames are a reminder of the distinctiveness of each individual. (3) That Daniel and his friends were away from home leads naturally into: the problems of loneliness, feelings of isolation, alienation. This may in turn lead to a consideration of: (4) prayer, meditation, thoughtfulness, and of the need to have moments alone for development of character and for spiritual growth. (For help in developing this section see Paul Tournier, *On the Meaning of Persons* and Henri Nouwen, *Reaching Out: The Three Movements of the Spiritual Life*.)

(B) Choosing a life style is an important decision. (1) There are a variety of life styles open to singles. (2) Some patterns may be deliberately rejected. (Daniel chose not to conform to the royal pressures.) (3) There is no such thing as a useless person. Each is distinctive—with particular talents and opportunities for service and witness. ("We, though many are one Body in Christ, and individually members of one another" [Rom 12:5].) (4) The calling of the church is to be a fellowship, a communion, a group which helps others to think of others—and of God's design for our lives.

(C) Continuing education is imperative. (1) The alternative to growth—at any age—is stagnation. (2) The way to praise God joyfully is not necessarily by withdrawal/non-activity. (3) With development of the mind, hobbies and self-giving, one may grow and help others at the same time. (4) There is a need for the church to be more sensitive to singles.

Yet a third sermon may be developed on the basis of these verses which might be called, "Beyond the Boundaries." In this sermon you might explore the concept of special seasons when, "they say," no holds are barred, such as the Saturnalia, Bachanalia, New Year's Eve, or Mardi Gras. At such times "society" allows a relaxation of the usual moral restraints. Thomas Mann in his novel *The Magic Mountain* explores the psychology of this phenomenon in a masterful description of the mood, conversations and mounting tempo of the masquerade ball. Harvey Cox's *Feast of Fools* discusses the theology of play. A sermon might be devoted to pointing out the importance, hazards, and limits of play when travel or relaxation of social restraints transports one "beyond the boundaries."

## Diet and Disposition (1:9–16)

To eat of the royal food evidently would have constituted a violation of food laws of the Torah. Daniel and his friends display initiative and persistence. They did not supinely surrender to "city hall." They sought a way to modify an objectionable regulation. The book of Daniel thus provides a model for individual social action and for seeking to change the regulations of the prevailing social order.

The motive behind abstinence from wine may be derived from the biblical prophets. Hosea taught that wine could dull the sensibilities so that one would more readily abandon God (Hos 4:11–12). Amos taught that, with a surfeit of wine, one might be led to commit callous acts against the poor (Amos 4:1). There is thus no teetotalism for the sake of teetotalism in the Bible. Reasons are given to show why drink is a poor master. The Bible is not, however, uniformly opposed to the imbibing of alcoholic beverages. The psalmist thanks God for "wine that gladdens the face of man" (Ps 104:15).

Awareness of the corrupting potential of luxurious food and wine is a well-known theme from antiquity given some prominence in Herodotus, the Cynic philosophers, and the Stoic philosophers. In setting forth this challenge to the Judaic life-style, the author could thus count on some sympathy from readers with Cynic or Stoic leanings. On the issue of abstinence there was common ground. A suitable pre-Lenten sermon, called "Diet and Disposition" might be developed along the following lines.

(A) Food affects disposition. (1) The food of Judeans had a favorable effect on their health. (The word translated "vegetables" in the RSV may have been "pulse," that is, edible seeds of leguminous plants such as peas, beans, and lentils.) (2) In other societies the relationship between diet and disposition, food and muscle tone, is recognized. (In India it is taught that some foods lead to a dull, sullen disposition, some to a fiery or greedy or argumentative disposition, and others to a purer and more serene disposition.)

(B) Not only type, but amount of intake, may affect weight. (1) Becoming overweight may be a particular problem of middle age and retirement. (2) Overeating is a subtle form of suicide.

(C) In the history of the people of God, how one handles the intake of food has varied and sometimes is used as an expression of, or means to facilitate, faith. (1) People in the first age from Creation to the Flood were non-carnivores (Gen 9:1–3). (2) The Bible teaches a relation between faith and eating: some foods are prohibited (Deut 14; Lev 11). (3) Doing without a noon meal on a regular basis (or a meal of bread and cheese) for Oxfam, Bread for the World, One Great Hour of Sharing, is a worthy way to express one's faith.

## Christians and Jews (1:17–21)

The concluding verses in this chapter stress how God is the ultimate source of all knowledge (v. 17), and how the four Judeans endowed therewith surpass in wisdom and understanding even the Babylonian "magicians" and "sorcerers" (Greek: "sophists" and "philosophers"!) (vv. 18–20). Four different words for knowledge are used in vv. 17 and 20: "understanding," "skill in books (and counting)," "wisdom," and "discernment." A helpful sermon could be preached on "The Kinds of Wisdom."

In the town where I was raised (Great Neck: located seventeen miles east of New York City), the population was a third Protestant, a third Catholic, and a third Jewish. I used to think that that is what all America is like. Perhaps because of my having been raised in such a manifestly pluralistic community, I see in these verses an opportunity for the preacher to address a subject of importance for many an urban and suburban community: "Christians and Jews." In such a sermon the preacher might wish to touch on the following points.

(A) Christians are indebted to, and have much in common with, members of the Jewish community. (1) The psalms, the prophets, the proverbs of the Old Testament are the foundation bequeathed to the Christian churches by the Jewish communities and their forebears. (2) The stress on education and its ultimate divine source apparent in Dan 1 is another legacy from Judaism and another deeply shared conviction. (Present day Jewish contributions to higher education and the cultural life of American communities are of immense proportions and of benefit to all.) (3) The commitment to justice—and working for it—has its origins in the prophets of the Old Testament. (In the civil rights movement and in protests against the imbalances of the war in Vietnam, Jewish leaders were courageous and prominent in insisting that life for no one can be fully human if the divine demand for justice is ignored and given only lip service.) (4) Jesus of Nazareth and Paul of Tarsus were steeped in the traditions and scriptures of Judaism. (Christians share with Jews an affirmation of the providence of God and of the sanctity of that part of the Bible which Christians call the Old Testament.)

(B) There are differences. (1) Christians find the Jewish food laws (observed by Orthodox and Conservative, but not Reform, Jews) difficult to understand. (2) And yet the food laws are biblical (Deut 14, Lev 11). (Rabbi Mordecai Waxman of Temple Israel in Great Neck used to ask me, partly jokingly, "Why don't you Christians keep the kosher food

laws if you say you are biblical?") (3) A brilliant defense of
the kosher food laws is found in the second century B.C. trea-
tise entitled, the *Letter to Aristeas*. (Animals that are rapa-
cious are not eaten—to instruct in the avoidance of rapacity
in human conduct. Animals that chew the cud—a symbol of
reflectiveness—and divide the hoof—a symbol of the importance of exercising intellectual discrimination—may be eat-
en: to instruct in the importance of reflection and of
intellectual discernment.) (4) Jewish persons have not accepted Jesus as saviour because they do not see the fulfillment of Scripture that the lion is lying down with the lamb,
or that the knowledge of God is covering the land, or that the
present era on earth—in which we Christians say the Messiah has come—is one of justice and equity. (See esp. Isa 9 and
11.) Yet the Bible says these things will happen when the
Messiah comes. (Christians respond: these idyllic times will
come only when Jesus returns.)

(C) How should we Christians relate to the Jewish community? (1) Some say: "Evangelize!" In the divine plan the
Jewish communities will be grafted back on to the tree from
which they have been cut off as a branch (Rom 9–11). (2)
Others say: "Dialogue! Discuss!" Efforts to evangelize are so
often patronizing and demeaning (both to evangelizer and to
the "target" of evangelization). (3) (No matter which position
is taken): From a biblical and practical point of view the
Christian community stands in a tremendous debt to the
Jewish community and its forebears and can hardly: (a) rest
at ease if Christian proclamation or teaching fosters anti-
Semitism; (b) take lightly any attack upon any member of
the Jewish community; (c) allow Christian outreach to become de-humanizing; (d) overlook the present contributions
of Jews to American intellectual, cultural, and moral life.

Following outmoded dietary laws, avoiding external
worship of an idol, remaining faithful in prayer may seem to
be so insignificant—and certainly not worth risking one's life
for, such as is described in 2 Maccabees 7, 4 Maccabees, Dan
3 and 6. A sermon would be in order "On the Seeming Folly
of Religious Rules." Examples could be taken from Daniel 1
and the above passages, and the point made that religious
rules and ritual may provide an essential clue for gaining insight into, and providing, a meaningful structure to exis-

tence. The sermon might conclude with this quotation from Norman Porteous, former Professor of Old Testament, New College, Edinburgh, Scotland: "In this strange world the good oftener than not does not survive by compromise however reasonable, but by adopting an extreme position and it is usually the men [persons] who stick to principle even in the matters which seem in the world's eyes of little moment who stand firm in the evil day when issues of consequence are involved" (*Daniel*, p. 19). For further development of this theme, see also suggested sermons in chapter six on "Prayer" and "The Risks of Commitment."

# The Enigmatic Dream
## (Daniel 2:1–49)

It is customary to preach a series of biblical sermons based on different books of the Bible or on different chapters of one book. Chapter two in Daniel might be an exception. The chapter easily falls into five episodes—not dissimilar to the melodrama of the old time Saturday morning movie serials—each one picking up, after a brief recapitulation, where the last one left off. Episode one (vv. 1–11) describes the king's unsettling dream and his request of his own enchanters to tell him his dream and its interpretation. When the enchanters ask him to tell the dream first and they will provide the interpretation, the king responds with the threat of death to them if they do not comply with his request. The episode ends with the enchanters again asking the king to tell the dream, his refusal and their declaring his request impossible for humans. Episode two (vv. 12–23) commences with the king's angry resolve to slay *all* the sages of the realm (including, therefore, Daniel and his friends) because no one can recite the dream or tell its meaning. The chief hangman then searches out Daniel and his companions. Even before the solution of the mystery is revealed to Daniel—as it is, in a vision of the night (v. 19)—Daniel asks for an appointment with the king to tell him its interpretation (v. 16). The episode ends with Daniel thanking God, the source of all wisdom, for the revelation (vv. 20–23). Episode three (vv. 24–35) opens with Daniel making a plea for the king to issue a stay of execution because he will show the king the desired dream and its interpretation. Daniel stresses how the king's enchanters could not unlock the mystery and duly gives his God the credit as the revealer of mysteries (vv. 27–29) before he relates to the king its content (vv. 31–35). Episode four (vv. 36–45) contains the explanation of the dream which had been previously related. Episode five (vv. 46–49) concludes with the king's paying homage to Daniel and offering him a high post which Daniel humbly declines in favor of his three companions whom the king appoints instead over the affairs of the province of Babylon. A series of sermons on the chapter might, on the one hand, seek to sustain the melodramatic suspense at the conclusion of each episode and, on the other hand, to explore the original and modern messages in these episodes. The element of suspense would derive, in part, of course, from the audience (congregation's) not knowing precisely where the preacher would be placing his/her interpretive emphasis.

## That Unsettling Dream/Is Scrooge Alive and Well? (2:1–11)

It is not entirely clear from the text of v. 3, "my spirit is troubled to know the dream," whether in the story the king has forgotten the dream or whether what is meant is that he wishes "to know" its meaning. In any event, the subject matter of dreams and the seemingly unyielding character of the king readily suggest themselves as sermon topics to be based on these verses. Under the topic "That Unsettling Dream" or "Dreams Before and After Freud," a sermon might be developed along these lines.

(A) Here is some background on the interpretation of dreams in the ancient Near East. (1) A recent study of dreams in the ancient Near East by the Austrian Assyriologist, A. Leo Oppenheim, distinguishes three main types: (i) dreams which are a revelation of the deity which may or may not require interpretation; (ii) dreams which reflect, symptomatically, the state of mind or the spiritual and bodily health of the dreamer; and (iii) mantic dreams in which forthcoming events are prognosticated. (2) Whereas in the ancient Near East the Babylonians were recognized for their expertise in astrology, the Egyptians were recognized for their expertise in dream interpretation. (The same Egyptian name of sooth-sayer priest [*hartom* = RSV "magician"] found in Dan 2:2, 10, 27 is also found in a text of the Assyrian king Esarhaddon of the 7th century BC.) (3) In the Old Testament (a) God (Elohim) uses dreams as a means to warn a Philistine king so he will not violate the marriage bed of the patriarch Abraham (Gen 20:1–7) and (b) Joseph, like Daniel, is successful in interpreting dreams which are at once messages from the deity and prognostications of events to come (Gen 40:1–41:57). (4) Dreams may come as a premonition of death (as to Enkidu in the famous Epic of Gilgamesh) or as a warning of events to come (as to Gilgamesh) or as a presaging of a restoration of health and favor with the divine (as in the famous poem of the so-called Babylonian Job, "I Will Praise the Lord of Wisdom"). (5) The meaning of the Akkadian *parasu*, usually translated "to interpret" with reference to dreams, is rather "to solve, explicate, explain, translate or remove (the evil consequences of)." Accordingly the meaning of the Aramaic *peshar* (Hebrew *patar*) usually translated "to interpret" very likely contains the same connotation. (The king in Daniel 2 thus asks not simply for a telling of the dream and "its interpretation" but rather its "translation, explanation or [even better] solution.")

(B) Here is how dreams were understood by Sigmund Freud and some of his successors. (1) Dreams are a reliable clue to wishes and fears repressed from conscious thought. (2) They are primarily sexual, even incestuous, in nature. (3) Despite certain excesses and needed correctives, Freud's theories have produced a significant return to interest in and study of dreams and their importance. (4) According to Freud's pupil, C. G. Jung, dreams provide insight into the "collective unconscious," a residue of human experiences, anxieties and fears handed on at the unconscious level from our forebears. (Some of the imagery and symbols of dreams recur, says Jung, transculturally in religious symbolism.) (5) Recent scientific studies of sleep show that dreams occur during the so-called REM (Rapid Eye Movement) phase of sleep. (Sounds heard during this phase may be incorporated into dreams.)

(C) God is Lord of the conscious and unconscious thought. (1) The biblical, and modern psychological, view of dreams are not as far apart as may appear. Both assert that dreams may inform us of aspects of our lives of which we may be only dimly aware. (2) The biblical emphasis on the predictive aspect of dreams and the Freudian (of dreams as expressive of wish-fulfillment and of fears) are not as far apart as may seem. (Unconscious wishes and fears have a way of being put into action—sometimes even against our conscious will, as St. Paul thoroughly understood: Rom 7:15–20). (3) The believer need not reject the insights of psychology into the meaning of dreams. More conscious of our anxieties and fears, we may the more directly and openly be able to deal with them.

Another sermon based on these verses might call attention to the unreasonableness of the demands of the king and compare it to the drive for perfection (and the attendant problems) among successful persons and people in positions of authority. Such a sermon might be entitled: "Is Scrooge Still Alive and Well?" and might consider the following.

(A) People upset tend to take it out on others. (1) Nebuchadnezzar in Dan 2:1–11 is an exaggerated version of a frequent recurrence. When people are upset they may: (a) demand of others an immediate solution to their problem; or (b) accuse others prematurely of nefarious motives or of defects in character if they do not immediately comply (see vv. 8–9). (2) Before the upset person takes it out on his/her spouse, children, peers at work, underlings at work, or animals, it may be well to analyze the source of the disturbance or irritation. (3) Even able people may need to reflect on the reasonableness of their demands and expectations of others ("Of the one to whom much has been given, much will be required": Luke 12:48).

(B) Persons in authority can make seemingly unreasonable demands. This presents a dilemma. (1) Bureaucratic achievers are frequently accused of being "autocrats," "tyrants." Yet without such demands of one's self and of others, far less would have been achieved. All of us can think of acquaintances or persons in the community who have achieved and stimulated others to success although they are tyrants. (2) Persons with considerable authority can make unreasonable, unattainable ulcer-giving, and sometimes even wrongheaded, demands (see v. 10).

(C) Style of leadership and personal relations need not follow the Nebuchadnezzar syndrome. (1) Success in business and in the professions may jeopardize family relationships (which also merit some time and effort). (2) The giving of money to offspring is no substitute for the giving of love, time, and some periods of undivided attention. (3) Prayer and common sense may aid decision-making with respect to troubled areas (v. 11).

## The Urge to Destroy/Anti-Intellectualism/ The Function of Praise and Thanksgiving (2:12–23)

In these verses a caricature is drawn of a king who reaches such a point of frustration and anger that he calls for the destruction of the very persons on whom the effective functioning of his kingdom depends. (The sages were the bureaucrats and diplomats of the realm as well as teachers.) In recent times the wholesale attack and attempted annihilation of the Indian population in Uganda by Idi Amin is a frighteningly similar historical example of such political power gone amok. (From my observations in East Africa in 1969, the Indian population performed important roles in business, banking, transportation, and retail merchandizing.) The American riots during the 1960's in the ghettos of Detroit and Watts, and the British riots of the summer of 1981 are also similar and sobering examples of the destructive force of frustration. Perhaps the most frightening example of all times of the urge to destroy was the demonic effort to exterminate all of the Jewish people from modern Europe. It is unfortunately not likely that a sermon on this topic will soon become dated. Such a sermon might be called "The Urge to Destroy."

(A) Consider the ubiquity and sources of the urge to destroy: (1) Frustration at: a troubling unknown, joblessness, failure; (2) the desire for revenge (vindictiveness): bitter memories of past mistreatment and persecution; (3) mistaken, misdirected and warped hatred (selecting a scapegoat: on racial grounds, on religious grounds, on grounds of differentness, strangeness—anti-Semitism); and (4) competition for goods, land and resources deemed to be essential for life.

(B) Is there a cure? The beginning of a cure will touch the intellect, and will include the following: (1) understanding one's own and others' frustration (reasoning that past failures do not mean doom or future failures; "failure" should be defined); (2) attempting to put one's self in the shoes of "enemies"; (3) analysis of the psychology of "scapegoatism"; and (4) the attempt to devise conflict-reducing agencies (the international court of justice, the United Nations, law courts, religious groups, councils of churches, and municipal com-

missions on human rights can be seen as examples of conflict-reducing agencies).

(C) There is a need to go deeper (to touch the will and
emotions). (1) This can be facilitated by a faithful preaching
and hearing of the message of the Cross: (a) The Cross is a
tragic reminder of how even accepted and respected bureau-
cracies and governments can destroy life in the name of justice, order, and expediency; (b) The urge to destroy is still
present, not only in others, but in us (even though for the moment, perhaps, held in check). (2) Can the heart be reached?:
(a) In "Christian" Northern Ireland—with Protestants and
Roman Catholics at one anothers' throats—can love replace
hatred?; (b) Grudge-bearing; (c) apathy; and (d) turning a
deaf ear are passive, yet clear, forms of the urge to destroy.
(3) What do we need to be sufficiently alarmed, awakened
from apathy, or committed to openness to the transforming
love of God?: (a) acknowledgement of the urge to destroy
within ourselves; (b) acknowledgement of the consequence
on others of our urge to destroy and vindictiveness; (c) repentance (whence does it come?); (d) acceptance of the divine
forgiveness of us; (e) forgiveness of others; this will mean not
simply forgetting, but caring enough to listen, to learn the
past history of previous foes (scapegoats), and learning to see
nobility of character in past foes. (See Alan Paton's moving
novel, *Cry, the Beloved Country*.)

A sermon on anti-intellectualism is a natural for this
chapter ("and the king commanded that all the wise men
should be destroyed") and may be more needed than we are
aware. Several decades ago Richard Hofstadter of Columbia
University wrote a book, *Anti-Intellectualism in America*, in
which he outlined how in revivalism and conservative religious groups of the far-right, even though the intellect is used
and reasoning valued, energies are often directed against edu-
cational institutions and institutions of higher learning. Discussion of and sermons on anti-intellectualism provide a good
opportunity for airing the important subjects of the relationship of faith, reason, religious liberty, and the freedom of
speech. At least some items to emphasize and ponder for such
a sermon would be: (i) The Great Commandment to love God
with the mind (Matt 22:37). (ii) Anti-intellectualism is frequently born of fear and a basic anxiety and distrust that the

truth of God will not in the long run prevail. (iii) Intellectual challenges to the faith may strengthen it; make it more mature and sensitive. (iv) For faith to speak to modern persons, we must vigorously seek to use the intellect to understand the modern world rather than merely being suspicious of modern developments. (v) Reason is no substitute for faith, yet the fear of the use of reason may itself be a needless lack of faith.

Another suitable sermon based on these verses—and especially vv. 20–23—would be: "The Function of Praise and Thanksgiving." The development of this sermon might take the following line.

(A) God may be praised. (1) As the source of wisdom and power (v. 20); (2) For His ordering of the seasons and providential superintending, even of the political order (v. 21); (3) As being the source of light, the knower even of the darkness and the revealer of mysteries (v. 22).

(B) Humankind was created for praise (Ephes 1:11–12) (1) Human well-being rests in fulfilling the role for which we have been created: to praise God with heart, mind, in work, worship, and service. (2) To dedicate self and talents to worthy goals, worthy beings, or worthy institutions is not the same as, though it may be a part of, the praise of God. (3) The praise of God will mean that all other loyalties—however high and noble—cannot be given an absolute status. (Church, family, nation, race, business organizations can command only proximate loyalties.) (4) Ultimate trust and ultimate praise belong alone to the Ultimate. (True commitment to, and love of, family, nation, one's own people cannot be made *at any cost*. That would be idolatry and renunciation of the praise of God.)

(C) Thanksgiving is a prime theological virtue. (1) Thanksgiving is not simply an act, but an attitude. (2) Learning to give thanks for the trials, hardships, anomalies, and mysteries of life is a part of the message of the Cross and of the calling to praise God (Rom 8:18–25; 11:20–36; 2 Cor 1:13–14; 5:1–15).

## The Purpose of Counsel/Premonitions of Demise and Displacement (2:24–35)

These verses naturally fall into two parts: Daniel before the king and his exchange with him (vv. 24–30) and Daniel's

telling the king the content of the king's (forgotten?) dream
(vv. 31–35). At least two sermons suggest themselves as appropriate reflections on the text. The first one might be
called "The Purpose of Counsel."

(A) There is a widespread call for counsel. (1) Among
family, friends, church, state, business there abides a need
for persons with wisdom, to advise and give counsel. (2) Each
of us wants to be able to give sound advice. (3) Educa-
tion/training may help. (4) But, wisdom's true source is God
(v. 30a).

(B) The purposes of wisdom are manifold: (1) to provide
explanations/solutions to human dilemmas (v. 30b); (On the
meaning of "interpretation" [peshar] as "solution," etc., see
the discussion of dreams at the beginning of this chapter); (2)
to help other human beings know and understand their own
thoughts (v. 30c); (3) to enable others to see in perspective
what appears to them as awesome responsibilities (v. 31);
and (4) to prepare others to recognize that even dearly loved
and precious institutions may pass, perish, or be transformed
(vv. 32–35).

A second sermon based on vv. 24–35 might be called,
"Premonitions of Demise and Displacement." The introduction might start out as follows. Death is inevitable. "The
years of our life," says the Bible, "are three score years and
ten or even by reason of strength, fourscore; yet their span is
but toil and trouble; they are soon gone and we fly away" (Ps
90:10). The older we get the more this pragmatic reality of
death presses in. Karl Barth, the great Swiss theologian
wrote in his 61st year, "The chances of life are ever diminish-
ing and its limitations loom ever larger." Slightly less than
200 years ago Samuel Johnson, the great man of letters, expressed to his friend James Boswell his awful dread and fear
of death. "The whole of life," he said, "is but keeping away
the thought of it." Instead of apologizing or being ashamed of
this fear, he championed it, "For the better a man is, the
more afraid he is of death, having a clearer view of infinite
purity." Development of the sermon might take the following
course.

(A) Dreams may be expressive of fears or dread of failure,
impending doom, or death. (1) The dream of Nebuchadnezzar was a premonition of the end of his kingdom and of its

replacement. (2) There is a simplicity and clarity to this symbolic premonition. (a) the gold, silver, bronze, etc. evaluate; (b) the stone cut with no human hand represents a divine agency; (c) the shattering and dispersal suggests a military conquest (in contrast to chapter 7); (d) the stone becomes a mountain, filling the earth—suggesting a highly successful political replacement. (3) This symbolic premonition is thus chiefly social and political in character.

(B) More personal images of death are found in the poem of Eccl 12:6–7. (1) The images are similar to those of Dan 2, but more explicitly individual: (a) snapping of the silver cord; (b) breaking of the golden bowl; (c) fragmenting of the pitcher at the fountain; (d) breaking down of the wheel at the cistern/well; (e) returning to dust; and, (f) return of the spirit to God. (2) Through a poem of such beauty we are aided in seeing: the preciousness of life and a plan and pattern even in death.

(C) The demise of institutions is reviewed and foreseen. (1) The focus in 2:24–35 is on the evaluation, shattering, dispersal, and replacement of a social institution. (2) In this instance, probably of the "death" of a national state (Ptolemaic Egypt) or a succession of national states (Babylon, Media, Persia, Greece) by another (probably Rome, "the stone that . . . became a great mountain").

## For Thine Is the Kingdom/Patterns in History (2:36–45)

There are two major differences between the content of the dream (vv. 31–35) and its interpretation/solution (vv. 36–45). The first is significant theologically, the second historically. In the dream itself nothing is said about the source of power or strength of the head of gold, as it is in its *peshar*/solution (vv. 36–38). In the dream itself the nature of the mixture of iron and clay in the feet of the image (v. 33) is not explained with as great detail as it is in the solution (vv. 41–43). Scholars differ on the identification of the four kingdoms—as we have just indicated in C. (2) of the sermon outline above. By the time of the apocryphal book of 2 Esdras, the fourth kingdom was no longer understood to be Greece, but Rome (2 Esdras 12:10–30). In my judgment, as I have argued elsewhere, the four parts of the single image were to the author of Dan 1–6 the four kings of the Greco-Egyptian (Ptolemaic) Empire which the author foresaw would soon be replaced by the might of Rome. The majority of scholars, however, take the parts to be politically separate kingdoms instead of four successive kings and reigns of the one empire. At least two sermons may be developed on these verses. The first "For Thine is the Kingdom" might treat the following topics.

(A) There is an element in the interpretive solution not in the dream: that God is the bestower of rule, power, might and glory. (1) This difference is part of the solution to the implied threat of the dream which explains how, at least in part, to remove its threatening aspect. (2) The clear teaching of the interpretive solution is that the king should not forget that God is the giver of power, etc. (see Deut 8:11–18).

(B) What is it that God gives? (1) Kingdom: (a) political rule (without disruptive riots or anarchy), (b) reign (control over the realm), and (c) democracy, as a fragile gift from God; (2) Might: (a) strength, (b) ability to withstand threats of other countries, (c) and dependency on God, not on military might alone; (3) Power: (a) wealth, (b) natural resources, and (c) developed resources; (4) Glory: (a) dignity, (b) reputation and esteem in the eyes of other nations.

(C) In proportion as the Source of these is remembered, they will endure. (a) They are not forever, but conditional. (2) The need remains to ask continually what the Sovereign requires by way of worship and justice (see Isa 5:16; Matt 25:31–46). (A concordance, theological dictionary and more detailed commentary will be especially helpful in developing section B. of the above suggested sermon.)

Another sermon on the periodization or patterns in history would seem to be a natural for this section. The dividing of history into periods begins formally in the Bible with the priestly writers who set forth four world ages: I—From Creation to Flood; II—From Noah to Abraham; III—From Abraham to Moses; and IV—The Mosaic Era. In each of the successive eras, the lifespan of human beings successively decreased and the preferred name for God shifted from Elohim (first two ages) to El Shaddai (third age) until the final revelation of the name Yahweh (fourth age). In the apocalyptic writings the periodization of history is carried one step further into prediction of a future political power (Dan 2) or of the succession of political rule by a supra-terrestrial, heavenly kingdom (Dan 7). Archaeologists, historians and students of culture also like to "periodize," that is, to divide up the past into typical ages. Metals in use are the singlemost important factor for naming archaeological eras in the ancient Near East: Chalcolithic (lit. Copper-stone) Age (c. 4500–3100 BC), Bronze Age (3100–1200 BC), Iron Age (1200–300 BC). The metals for the ages in Dan 2 may go back to the Greek poet and student of mythology, Hesiod (c. 700 BC) who in his *Works and Days* speaks of five world ages—the fifth being an age of heroes which he placed between his Bronze and Iron Ages. Periodization, no matter who the periodizer, should be seen as an attempt to analyze, evaluate, understand, and hence to manipulate conceptually human history. A sermon on periodization in history would be suitable for the Fouth of July or for the birthday of any national hero. The following sermon outline is offered as a hypothetical example of how one might develop the theme: "The American Image."

(A) The Golden Age in America lasted from colonization to independence. It was characterized by: (1) religious commitment (e.g, the Mayflower Compact and Massachusetts Bay Colony); (2) religious pluralism (Maryland with its Catholicism; Pennsylvania with its Quakerism; Rhode Island with its Anabaptism); and (3) a firm religious basis of government and commitment to human rights (Declaration of Independence). (4) During this period one might say that the head of gold was George Washington.

(B) The Silver Age in America lasted from the union to the Civil War. (1) During this period the head of silver was Thomas Jefferson; (2) In it the form of government matured (Constitution, Bill of Rights). (3) It also knew, however, sad moments such as the mistreatment of Indians under Andrew Jackson (Trail of Tears). (4) It was a period of expansion of borders from coast to coast, and (5) of increasing tension over slavery.

(C) The Bronze Age in America lasted from the Civil War to the advent of the auto. (1) During this period the head of bronze was Abraham Lincoln. (A southern congregation may wish to substitute Robert E. Lee. Reference could be made to

Stone Mountain outside of Atlanta rather than to Mt. Rushmore on which the four "heads" of this outline are sculpted.) (2) Tragic divisions (economic and ideological) took place before and after the war. (3) It was the time of the industrial revolution; railroad tracks stretched from coast to coast. (4) The impact of one or more of the great ideas from overseas was beginning to be felt (Marx, Nietzsche, Darwin, and Freud).

(D) The Age of Iron and Clay in America lasts from 1900 to the present. (1) In it we might say the head of iron was Theodore Roosevelt (conservationist). (2) This was the age of conservationism and the large-scale establishment of national parks and (3) large-scale manufacture of the automobile (Henry Ford—1908). (4) This was the age of wars: WWI, WWII, Korea, Vietnam. (5) This is the age of electronic expansion (radio, TV, calculators, computers) and (6) attempts to cope with the clay (internal weaknesses): civil rights, riots, inflation, recession, and spiritual deterioration.

(E) Is there a stone not made by human hands on the horizon? (1) Possible causes for a divine judgment or cultural degeneration which might be cited are: (a) failure to implement our avowed ideal of justice; (b) our extravagant lifestyle and excessive consumption of the world's resources (6% of the world's population in America and the developed nations annually utilizes 40% of the total resources consumed); (c) failure to see our nation as but one nation in a family of nations ("The Arrogance of Power": Senator William Fulbright); and (d) failure to recognize the Source of Power. (2) Will a divine judgment also come on our nation? (3) (To the congregation): "What will your role be in this American image?" (For inspirational and informative reading on this topic see Sydney E. Ahlstrom's very readable *A Religious History of the American People.*)

## Athens Turns to Jerusalem (2:46–49)

These four verses are among the most unusual verses of Scripture. They rank in difficulty in preaching subject, in my opinion, with the exorcism from the man named Legion of evil spirits who get leave from Jesus to enter a herd of swine which thereupon promptly rushes headlong into the sea to be drowned (Mark 5:1–13). In these last verses in Dan 2 the king "falls upon his face," "does homage to Daniel," and "commands that an offering and incense be offered up to him" (v. 46)—acts that are surely more appropriate before God than before another human being! The king does praise Daniel's God as "God of gods" (v. 47), so the unusual actions of v. 46 are almost explainable. Almost. Such actions by foreigners are prophesied in Isaiah of Babylon (see Isa 45:14 NEB). It is thus possible that these verses were added to Daniel to show here that the kind of prophecies made during the Exile were subsequently being fulfilled among Judean courtiers whose task it was to bring foreign kings to acknowledge the supremacy of "the God of gods"—as they also do elsewhere in Daniel (4:1-3, 34-35; 6:26-27).

A sermon might be developed on the task of the church and synagogue to make secular leaders (at Athens) aware of the limits of their power as well as of the spiritual resources (at Jerusalem). In this sermon Athens stands for an areligious, chiefly secular, culture and Jerusalem for Judeo-Christian culture and commitment. The sermon might be called, "The Love-Hate Relationship of Athens to Jerusalem."

(A) There is an anti-religious (and anti-clerical) bias of at least some intellectuals, business, and political leaders. (Many in Athens think there is little good to come from Jerusalem—and what there is is muddle-headed.) (1) This bias is discernible in some departments at some universities. (2) Some great writers such as A. Solzshenitsyn are held to be less than great because their depth of commitment is equated with fanaticism.

(B) There is an awareness also among some intellectuals, business, and political leaders of: (1) the need to acknowledge that church and synagogue and their insistence on the divine dimension of life have something of importance to say even to—or especially in—a technological age, because of: (2) the past and present failures of technology to control the mechanisms of destruction; and (3) the inadequacy of simply naturalistic views of human nature in contrast to the profundities of the view of human nature present in scripture and theistic theologies; and (4) the limits and demonic dimensions of a technologically-focused materialism unchecked by a theologically-based morality. (Others in Athens are aware that Athens needs Jerusalem.)

(C) Church and synagogue leaders—not simply clergy—have a responsibility to realize afresh the depth of the resources in the biblical and theistic faith. (1) Man (humankind) cannot live by bread and technology alone. (2) Destructive forces within must be acknowledged, curbed, and re-directed to more peaceful and life-building ends. (3) Some profound views of human nature in Scripture are: (a) one can end up hating the very one whom one has (previously desired and) exploited (e.g, Amnon of Tamar: 2 Sam 13); (b) the mood in human beings of great despondency—even of the "successful"—should be acknowledged (Ps 42—43); (c) no over-simplified analysis of the reason for the mood shift from despondency to exultation, found so frequently in the psalms of lamentation, can be given: but it is an unmistakable fact of spiritual life (see Pss 6, 51, 102, 130); (d) human beings possess both a base and a noble, a bestial and a self-transcending, aspect (see Pss 8, 57; B. Paschal, *Pensées*; Reinhold Niebuhr, *Nature and Destiny of Man* and G. Buttrick's "Exposition" of Matt 5-7 in *The Interpreter's Bible*). (4) Materialism which places acquisition of goods and self-gratification as the highest goods is doomed to failure. (If Athens which has sold out unwittingly to materialism or scientism has some misgivings about its own limitations and turns to Jerusalem, as Nebuchadnezzar does to Daniel and his God, there is hope.)

For further ideas on the relationship of Jerusalem and Athens, see above my comments on 1:1–4 and below on 3:1–12 and 4:13–27.

# Eloquent Pagan/Miraculous Deliverance
## (Daniel 3:1–30)

There are a number of important theological themes beautifully illustrated in this chapter: (i) the power of God to save and deliver even from the most difficult of circumstances; (ii) how to live in a pagan culture when the pressures for conformity are severe; (iii) how a pagan moves from intolerance to tolerance of the non-worship of his own state gods; (iv) the risks of commitment; (v) the cost of discipleship; (vi) the courage of faithfulness; and (vii) how fidelity is rewarded. A sermon on any one or combination of these subjects would be in order.

This theologically potent chapter is also potentially divisive. Perhaps the best clue on how to deal with the chapter should be taken from the text itself. The author had a keen sense of humor and a deep faith—both of which enabled him to poke mild fun at human pretensions and status seeking. If the preacher can emulate these two aspects in the chapter, I suspect it won't matter much how other issues are decided. The issues are nonetheless serious.

Should the preacher insist that every last member of the congregation know the correct form-critical classification of the story? Scholars differ in the precise classification of the chapter. Some say it is a "legend" or "tale" told to incorporate and illustrate the truth of the scriptural sentences of Isa 43:2: "When you pass through the waters, I will be with you, and through the rivers, they shall not overwhelm you; when you walk through fire you shall not be burned, and the flame shall not consume you." Others say it is an "aretalogy" told to extol the glorious deeds, wonders, or miracles (*aretai*) of God. Others say it is a typical "martyr story" told not so much to demonstrate the divine power to work miracles but rather with the end in view of inculcating steadfastness of faith and an unswerving witness (*martyria*) in the face of persecution. Others say it is a "romance," similar to pagan romances of the Hellenistic period, which as a matter of literary convention, typical to other pagan romances, contains a story of the deity's faithfulness to protect those devotees who are loyal to him/her. Others suggest it be classified as a "court tale of contest" because it highlights the strife between the Babylonian and Judean courtiers. And, still others hold that the account is factually accurate, literally true and therefore a reliable report of a miraculous event that actually transpired. Whether the preacher should inform his/her congregation of this range of scholarly discussion will depend on the preacher's own decisions on these matters and on his/her estimate of the cultural sophistication of the congregation. (The feisty Henry Sloane Coffin, former President of Union Theological Seminary in New York once said in my hearing, "The ability of a person to accept and assimilate the findings of the Higher Criticism of the Bible will vary directly in proportion to his education and sophistication.")

No matter what the classification of the chapter, it contains the same structure of the other stories in chapters 1–6. The chapter might also be likened to a three-act drama. Act one, scene one: the king erects a golden image and invites all his officials to its dedication (vv. 1–3). Scene two: the herald proclaims that all who do not fall down and worship the image at the sound of music will be cast into a furnace. Envious Babylonian court officials thereupon charge three Judeans with non-conformity with the proclamation (vv. 4–12). Act two, scene one: the king, in a rage, summons the recalcitrant three and gives them a second chance. They defiantly respond that they have no need to answer the king in this matter and boldly state their confidence that their God will deliver them, but even if not, they will not comply (vv. 13–18). Scene two: the order is given for the three to be cast into a furnace heated seven times hotter than usual. The Persians who threw them into the furnace died from the heat and the three tumble in, bound, and fully clothed in Persian costume (vv. 19–23). Act three, scene one: the king sees the three walking in the furnace unharmed, and an unidentified fourth figure with them (vv. 24–25). Scene two: the king orders them out, and upon seeing that they are not so much as singed or smelling of smoke, he issues a decree swearing death to anyone who speaks anything against such a God who can so deliver. As a final action in the story he promotes the three

(vv. 26–30). In sum, the pagan king who at the beginning of the drama insists upon the worship of his image of gold, ends in eloquent acknowledgment of the wondrous power to save of the God of Shadrach, Meshach, and Abednego. Miraculous deliverances are a convention, a regular feature, in Hellenistic romances and aretalogies. Such also seems to have been the case with Dan 3. The point of the story was certainly not to undermine the faith of the faithful nor to weaken their determination to resist idolatry. The opposite is the case. The validity of the teaching of this story on the faithfulness of God remains firm and the story itself is an eloquent witness of the author's faith. Surely we would not wish to take away from the biblical writers their right to tell stories because the events described did not literally happen. Would we take away from Jesus the right to tell the parable of the Good Samaritan because no specific persons literally did perform the acts described in the parable? The deep spiritual truths of stories such as this, as of the parables of Jesus, are not so much dependent upon a direct relationship to literal happenings as they are upon the author's ability to resonate with ultimate reality and to perceive ultimate verities beneath and beyond the literal. (For modern day examples, see C. S. Lewis, *The Chronicles of Narnia*, or J. R. R. Tolkien's moving trilogy, *Lord of the Rings*, where an entirely fictitious "hobbit" is shown to be a model of self-sacrificing heroism.)

## The Dimensions of Idolatry (3:1–12)

Nebuchadnezzar constructed an image of gold in the valley of Dura. The valley of Dura has not been located by archaeologists, yet the city of Sargon II, Dur-Sharrukin ("Fortress of Sargon") in upper Mesopotamia has been excavated, and Dura-Europos is the site of a famous synagogue located near the ancient Mari on the Euphrates River. The dimensions of the image, sixty cubits by six cubits, is approximately ninety feet by nine feet. The dimensions of the image were remarkably close to those of the ancient Egyptian obelisks which, were often plated with gold and electrum, an alloy of gold and silver. Typical dimensions were: $x$ by $x$ (base) by $10x$ (height); the whole was surmounted by a pyramid. (The Washington Monument, an obelisk, has dimensions of 55' x 55' x 555'. Building of the monument ceased during the

Civil War and the color of the stone used after the war does
not match exactly the antebellum stone. The monument thus
serves also as an eloquent monument of the tragic war between the states. Washington, D.C. is, of course, also the
home of the national bureaucracy such as the one spoofed in
vv. 3 and 4.) A sermon on "The Dimensions of Idolatry"
would be in order.

(A) The biblical and theological prohibition of idolatry is
plain. (1) Definition: idolatry may be defined as worship of
an idol (any thing, person, or social institution other than
God); (2) Citations: Biblical passages which speak against
idolatry are: (a) the first two of the Ten Commandments (Exod 20:3-6); (b) the Great Commandment (Matt 22:34-40);
and (c) prophetic satires on idol worship (Isa 40:18-20; 41:7;
44:9-20; 46:5-7; Jer 10:1-16).

(B) Modern idols: to what depths and height do they
reach? ("Where your treasure is there will your heart be also": Matt 6:21.) (1) Racism (exalting one's race above others):
consequences: enslavement of other human beings, genocide.
(For a devastating documentation of American racism, see H.
Sheldon Smith's *In His Image But . . . Racism in Southern Religion, 1780-1910*.) (2) Sexism (exalting of one's sex, usually
male, above the other): consequences: attempt to keep the
other sex subservient, contrary to the clear biblical teaching,
"In Christ there is neither Jew nor Greek, there is neither
slave nor free, there is neither male nor female; for you are
all one in Christ Jesus" (Gal 3:28). (3) Nationalism (uncritical
adulation of one's own nation): consequences: attempted or
actual suppression of neighboring nations, war. (For further
thoughts on the difference between patriotism and nationalism, see also the sermons suggested below on 4:1-18 and
12:1-3.) (4) Totalitarianism (deification of a system of government, whether of communism or fascism): consequences:
suppression of dissidents, deification of leaders, oppression
or perversion of theistic religion. (5) Militarism (exaltation of
armed force as the supreme way to settle human conflicts):
consequences: escalating arms races, underestimate or ne-
glect of non-violent means of settling internal or international differences. (6) Materialism (the exaltation or worship of
mammon, i.e., money, material wealth or social status and
prestige): consequences: treating people as less than human,

as pawns and means to an end, rather than as ends in themselves. Variations: (a) lust for power; (b) greed; (c) Jesus' response: "You cannot worship God and money" (Matt 6:24 NEB); (d) Response of pastoral epistles: see 1 Tim 6:10. (7) Scientism (exaltation of knowledge as the singlemost important human goal): consequences: creation of false hopes, frequent anti-religious bias, failure to reach and respond to basic human emotions.

(C) Common features of idolatries are: (1) the exaltation of self; (2) the urge to dominate others and control other human beings; and (3) the tendency to use the arts and public media as instruments of propaganda (in at least the first five noted above).

(D) Divine judgment stands over and against idolatry— of whatever form. (1) Idolatry of whatever sort contains within it the seeds of its own defeat. (2) This self-destructive and inevitably perverting aspect of idolatry was recognized and eloquently expressed in: (a) the canonical Scriptures (Rom 1:18–32); (b) the so-called deutero-canonical or apocryphal Scriptures (Wisdom of Solomon 16–19); and (c) theology (see esp. St. Augustine's *The City of God* and Reinhold Niebuhr's *The Nature and Destiny of Man*). (3) This sermon might close with a citation of Jesus' response to Satan when he promised Jesus "all the kingdoms of the world and the glory of them" (Matt 4:8–10).

A series of two or three sermons might easily be preached under the subject: "The Lure of Idolatry" on nationalism, militarism, etc. which could carry over from one Sunday to the other to emphasize and reinforce the point: the worship of any thing, person, or social institution other than God is idolatry.

## A Willingness to Suffer (3:13–23)

In this second act, Shadrach, Meshach and Abednego express a willingness to suffer—even to die—on behalf of their faith, rather than to bow down before the king's golden image or worship his gods (vv. 16–18). A series of three sermons on suffering would be natural developments from these verses. The series on suffering might be called "Out of the Depths" and the first sermon in the series could be called "The Fruit of Suffering."

(A) Eloquent words in Scripture, religious song, and literature have been written in times of exile, persecution, or imprisonment: (1) from the time of the Babylonian Exile (Ps 137, Ezekiel, Jeremiah, Isa 40—55, the editing of Deuteronomy through 2 Kings, the Priestly Source of the Pentateuch, and Lamentations); (2) from indeterminate periods of intense personal and perhaps social affliction (Pss 56, 57, 102, 130, etc.; Job); (3) from times of increasing persecution under the Ptolemies (Dan 1—6) and the Seleucids, during the Maccabean Revolt (Dan 7—12); and (4) from Roman times of persecution and threats of more (Mark, John, Philippians, Revelation). (5) To this list might be added: religious literature and music composed during periods of imprisonment, enslavement, or subjugation (John Bunyan's *Pilgrim's Progress*; Negro spirituals; M. K. Gandhi's *Autobiography*; M. L. King, Jr.'s "Speeches" and "Letter from a Birmingham Jail").

(B) The biblical literature born of suffering speaks to us in our suffering. (1) Or, is ours of a different sort? (2) Because born of surfeit and satiation rather than privation and pain?

(C) If, unlike the biblical examples and others just listed, we are not suffering from physical abuse, enslavement or imprisonment, we can learn to empathize, and thus: (1) become more sensitive to the pain of others; (2) become more aware of the extent of the blessings we have received; (3) learn to care, and (4) desire to share.

A second sermon in the series "Out of the Depths" could focus on the theme, "Biblical Responses to Suffering."

(A) From the Scriptures of the Old Testament we learn: (1) Suffering and calamity may be sent by God on humankind *as a punishment* for its wrong-doing, e.g., (a) Assyria, the rod of Yahweh's anger (against Israel) (Isa 10:5) and (b) the biblical notion of solidarity of the generations teaches: if an individual does not suffer for the wrong he/she has done, his/her offspring will (Exod 20:5; Sirach 30:4–6). (2) God uses suffering to *test* the faith of the sufferer (Job 1—2 and Dan 12:10). (3) God sends it to *teach* humankind about itself, about life, and about God what it cannot learn otherwise. (In this regard the book of Job is similar to the view of the Greek tragedies and to Shakespeare's *King Lear*.) (4) God identifies with humanity in its suffering and has deep compassion (lit.

"feeling with") so that He either: (a) provides the sufferer
with a way to cope with it (as in Job) or (b) will Himself in-
tervene to deliver the afflicted ones from their evil plight (as
in the exodus).

(B) From the Scriptures of the New Testament we learn:
(1) through Jesus God has fully identified with the human
predicament of suffering, pain, and woe: (a) in the incarnation (lit. "infleshment" [of the Word]) and (b) in the crucifixion. (2) An entire new perspective may be put on suffering in
that God has sent Jesus to be a model for the perfect life of
self-giving love. (This is the so-called Moral View of the
Atonement, e.g., John 13:34 and Peter Abelard.) (3) In Jesus,
God combats the Evil One (Satan) head-on. His crucifixion
and resurrection were crucial victories in the battle against
evil (just as the battles of El Alamein and Stalingrad were
turning-points, decisive victories, in World War II, so were
the crucifixion and resurrection decisive victories in the ultimate conflict with forces of evil). (This is the so-called Dramatic or Classic View of the Atonement, e.g., the gospel of
Mark, Col 1:13, and Martin Luther; see Gustav Aulen, *Chris-
tus Victor* and Oscar Cullmann, *Christ and Time*.) (4) Jesus
has become a substitution for humanity, taking its place as
an object of God's wrath on human cruelties and wrong-doing. Through His vicarious suffering, the divine demand for
justice has thus been satisfied. (This is the so-called Substitu-
tionary or Satisfactionary View of the Atonement, e.g., Rom
5, 2 Cor, Anselm, and Protestant orthodoxy.)

(C) In varying times and ages Christians have turned to
these responses to help them to explain the anomalies of suffering which have arisen from human or natural sources.

A third sermon in the series "Out of the Depths" might
address the topic, "A Willingness to Suffer."

(A) The pressures toward idolatry in 3:13-23 were more
direct and less subtle than contemporary pressures. (1) For
some reflections on the nature of idolatry see above on
3:1-12. (2) Our pressures come from the peer group (see D.
Riesman's *The Lonely Crowd*) or from the necessities of the
job (see C. Wright Mills' *The Power Elite*). (3) Seldom is the
alternative put as starkly for us as it is here, as if it were a
matter of physical death. (4) The consequences of contemporary idolatry will more likely be a slow, spiritual death.

(B) One might argue that compromise would seem to be the best policy (stated with deliberate irony): (1) it will ruffle fewer feathers; (2) everyone knows you are an honest person; (3) people feel deeply about it (race, national loyalty, military armaments, etc.), so it would be easier in this case to "bend a little" and "not create any waves." (4) All such pressures to compromise force upon us the *ordering* of our loyalties and setting of priorities. (Where does loyalty to God and His demands for uprightness, justice, peace and compassion stand among these? Or, are such concepts out of date and only the domain of the "bleeding-heart liberals"?) (5) Loyalty to God and the rejection of idolatry may be costly in terms of social influence, advancement, or acceptance. (People feel if you reject their idols you reject them and that you are pointing an accusing finger at them, their life-style and their values.)

(C) In the resolve not to compromise, there must be a willingness to suffer and an awareness that a meaningful spiritual life is simply impossible without commitment. (1) Because the pressures in contemporary Western society are subtler it is all the more necessary in lesser decisions to ask where is any one decision apt to lead if amplified or if more of the same kind of decisions are made. (2) Unwillingness to suffer for the sake of loyalty to God or a placing of other loyalties higher than the Great Commandment (Matt 22:34–40), may lead to spiritual suffering of a subtle, but very real sort: lack of a sense of meaning and direction in life even in the midst of material plenty, the pursuit of pleasure followed by boredom or self-hatred. (3) Is one of the secrets of "life" after all wrapped up in the willingness to suffer? (see Luke 9:23–24; John 10:10).

## The Holocaust: Past and Present (3:24–30)

In the same way that a fruitful comparison might be made between the text of Daniel and the contemporary scene, such as was suggested in the previous sermon outline, so a helpful, but perhaps painful, comparison might be made between these verses and the immense suffering of the Jews under Hitler in the ovens of Dachau, Auschwitz, and Buchenwald. The sermon might well be the fourth in a series on suffering. An appropriate time for preaching this sermon would

be Passion Sunday, or in April on the Sunday nearest to Yom
Ha-Shoah, Day of the Destruction. The horror of the slaughter of innocent Jewish men, women, and children in this century was so great, I am convinced that unless Christian
pastors, laity and theologians acknowledge its horrible reality and attempt to fathom it, we or our posterity will be
doomed to an irrevelant doctrine of the sufferings of Christ
and also, inevitably, to repetitions of such wholesale and unspeakable genocide. This topic could be addressed under the
rubric, "The Holocaust: Past and Present."

(A) The story in Dan 3 has a happy ending; the more
modern story of Jewish suffering does not. (1) It is painful to
recall the horrors of the Holocaust under Hitler. (2) So painful that some persons have sought to deny that six million
Jewish persons lost their lives in the concentration camps of
Auschwitz, Buchenwald, Dachau, Treblinka, Belsen, etc. (3)
The evidence of survivors, from the camps themselves, and
from the testimony of former Nazi officials at the Nuremberg
trials makes the fact of the Holocaust undeniable—unspeakable though it is. (4) The writings of Elie Wiesel (*The Oath,
Night, Dawn, The Testament*), Patrick White (*Riders in the
Chariot*), Anne Frank (*Diary*), Emil Fackenheim (*God's Presence in History*) and the records and remains of the former
Synagogue in Danzig all bring home the magnitude of Nazi
persecution of Jews and of the Nazi design systematically to
exterminate the Jewish people in what they called "The Final Solution."

(B) The roots of anti-Semitism are deep. (1) Although
Jesus, Paul, and the early disciples were all Jewish, the New
Testament itself says sufficient words about "the Jews" to
have fed the image that members of successive Jewish communities were "Christ-killers" (see especially John 8, 18—
19). (2) Even churchmen, churchwomen, and biblical scholars of the past and present century have been explicitly anti-
Semitic. (3) Christian dramatic presentations of the crucifixion still foster the notion that "the Jews are Christ-killers"
(e.g., Oberammergau). (4) Envy, frustration, unemployment,
inflation, and the idolization of the (Aryan) race and of the
nation have also fueled the fires of anti-Semitism.

(C) To assert that present-day Jewish suffering and
pogroms emanated out of divine judgment (because of the

denial of the Messiahship of Jesus, and because of Jewish involvement in the crucifixion) is self-deceptive, cruel, and sub-
Christian. (1) Anti-Semitism has roots in the baseness of
human nature and in idolatry. (2) Christians are called now
to search out their complicity and involvement in anti-Semitism. (3) The recent sufferings and wholesale slaughter of the
Jewish people in Europe should be lamented, and Christian
involvement acknowledged and repented of, if further divine
judgment on Christianity itself is to be averted. (4) In the
Holocaust, Christians have crucified their Lord afresh. (5)
There is a pressing, current need for churchpersons, theologians, and pastors to think out the significance of the sufferings of Christ in the light of the recent sufferings and death of
the descendants of Shadrach, Meshach, and Abednego.

# Models for Monarchy
## (Daniel 4:1—5:31)

Chapters four and five present two models for the conduct of secular kings: one positive (chapter four), the other negative (chapter five). Whereas Nebuchadnezzar demonstrates deference to, humility before, and receptivity to, the Most High God, His glorious deeds and counsel, Belshazzar shows contempt of the Most High through desecration of the temple vessels and praise of pagan gods. The two are rewarded in accordance with their respective deserts: Nebuchadnezzar is established in his kingdom and greatness is added to him (4:36) whereas Belshazzar dies (5:30).

To facilitate the contrast the fourth chapter of Daniel contains a minor variation in the sequence of typical elements in the stories of Dan 1—6. It commences with Nebuchadnezzar's general decree which at once praises the Most High for His wonders and announces the King's decision to tell the nations in the tale that follows what wonders have been unfolded before him (vv. 1–3). Not accidentally and in accordance with the typical sequence of episodes, the chapter closes with the king's praise of "the God of heaven" (v. 37).

In both chapters the Babylonian magicians fail and Daniel alone shows himself able to provide a *peshar*, i.e., an interpretation and solution to the threats contained within the dream and the riddle.

## Signs and Wonders (On Miracles)/Intimations of the Kingdom (4:1–3)

These verses should be read with vv. 34–37 (perhaps omitting from v. 34 the phrase "and my reason returned to me"). Two sermons would be appropriate. The first might be called "Signs and Wonders."

(A) The conclusions one draws about the miracles in the Bible are in many ways determined by how one defines "miracle." It is helpful to note at the outset that several words for "miracles" occur in the Old Testament—none meaning precisely "miracles" and each containing an important additional overtone: *othoth* ("signs"), *mophoth* ("portents") and *niphaloth* ("wonders"). In the New Testament the word *semeion* (pl. *semeia*) carries the double connotation of "sign" and "miracle," and the word *dynamis* carries the double connotation of "power" and "miracle." The major types of definitions of miracle are: (1) the rationalistic definition: "an event inconsistent with or in violation of the laws of nature"; (2) the religious definition: "an extraordinary event intended by God as a supernatural sign"; and (3) the (more neutral) phenomenological definition: "that which causes wonder and astonishment, being extraordinary in itself and inexplicable by normal standards." People will be drawn to one definition or another depending upon their previous training, disposition and background.

(B) Miracles have been the object of heated controversy since the Enlightenment. (1) Since the Enlightenment, or Age of Reason (1687–1750), attacks have been made on the credibility of the Bible on the basis of the miracle stories in both testaments. (2) Religion has taken several different tacks in response to the attacks of reason. (a) Defense has been made of the facticity and authenticity of the miracles. Or (b) it has been stressed that many miracles were not in violation of laws of nature but were extraordinary because of the timing of their happening (so B. W. Anderson in explaining the moving back of the waters of the Red Sea at the exodus). (c) It has been asserted that some New Testament miracles are characteristic of the New Creation, e.g., Jesus' walking on water and His resurrection. (With Jesus, for a brief moment, the laws of the "Old Creation" were set aside; so C. S. Lewis in *The Miracles*.) (d) It has also been stressed that, regardless of the facticity, the miracle accounts of both testaments contain tremendously important moral and theological lessons for the present. (Argued very persuasively for the New Testament by Alan Richardson in *The Miracle Stories of the Gospels*.) (e) These positions are not mutually exclusive. (3) Reason has tended to dictate the terms of the debate, focusing on whether or not the respective miracles of the miracle stories did occur.

(C) The facticity of the miracles—whether or not they happened exactly as recorded—should not be the primary

issue. (1) The primary issue pertains to the question of God:
"If one believes in God, that God creates the universe, sustains it, controls it, most of the difficulties of miracles have
thereby been dealt with. One who believes in God will believe in the possibility of miracles" (Vernon McCasland in
*The Interpreter's Dictionary of the Bible*). (2) The believer
may observe: (a) that belief in miracles is virtually always
accompanied by religious faith in God (or gods), and (b)
that reports of miracles cluster around all great religious
leaders (Moses, Buddha, Jesus, Mohammed). (3) Yet, from
the point of view of the Bible (a) the miracle is a sign of the
divine authority of the performer of the miracle(s) (Moses
with a wondrous rod turns water to blood, Exod 7:17–24;
Elijah in having greater effect in causing his God to answer
with fire from heaven to consume water-soaked sacrifices, 1
Kings 18; Jesus in turning water to wine, John 2); yet even
more importantly (b) the miracle accounts of both testaments point beyond themselves and the miracle performer
to the power and majesty and wonder of God and the presence or coming of His kingdom (Dan 4:1–3, 34–35; 6:26–27;
Luke 11:20).

A second sermon based on 4:1–3 might explore "Intimations of the Kingdom." In the introduction to this sermon the
preacher might note (i) the subject of the "kingdom," so important in the preaching of John the Baptist and Jesus, is giv-
en a particular prominence in Dan 2, 4, 6 and 7; (ii) careful
attention to the kingdom in Daniel may thus prepare the way
for a fuller understanding of the kingdom in the preaching of
Jesus. The rest of the sermon might then take the following
shape.

(A) In the story of Dan 4, King Nebuchadnezzar, a ruler
of an earthly kingdom, comes to an awareness of the existence of another kingdom through the awful experience of
having his kingdom cut off and himself experiencing a
mental breakdown. (1) The story is a parable of how out of
loss may come gain, out of defeat a renewed zest for life, out
of mental trials and disarray an added security (v. 36) and
tranquility (v. 27). (2) The king learns the hard way. Deprivation, loss of rule, loss of "one's grip on life," loss of reason for
a time, all contribute to the king's awareness that, from the
perspective of eternity, any earthly rule is fleeting. (3) After

his experience, the king praises God; his praise focusses on God's signs and wonders (vv. 2–3) and on His divine power to issue decrees which no human can alter (v. 35). (The former reason for praise includes not only the "sign" of the reception of the dream, its interpretation and its actual fulfillment, but also the "wonder" at what he has gained from his experience.)

(B) The lesson of the story is that through humility the king gains insight into the present and everlasting kingdom of God of which he had previously been entirely unaware. (1) With eyes opened to God's everlasting kingdom and of his own ephemeral power, Nebuchadnezzar also discerns how the rule of God is not something abstract or of the future, but a present reality which endures from generation to generation. (2) The king also now sees that above earthly kings there is a sovereign king, the Most High God (v. 2) who does not simply make decrees arbitrarily, but to teach earthly kings and to instruct them (v. 25). (3) Over and against this sovereign king, earthly power is limited, deficient, vulnerable and fleeting. (4) Through his suffering he has attained a wisdom which others recognize. Ironically, one who comes to such an awareness—(i) that human kings last for only a generation; (ii) that human kings have other weak spots; (iii) that there is an eternal kingdom—turns out to be one whom even "counselors" and "lords" seek out (v. 36). (5) The moral of the story: the only real way up is down.

(C) The teaching of Jesus on the kingdom, and later, of St. Paul, builds upon the concepts of Daniel. (1) That the meek shall inherit the earth (Matt 5:5) is already found in Dan 4 (see also Zeph 3:11–13). (At least one of the meanings of this beatitude is that the rulers [and followers] who practice humility will have greater staying power on earth than the arrogant. For striking historical illustrations of the validity of this teaching, see Herbert Butterfield's *Christianity and History*.) (2) Jesus teaches that God is king in the parable of the king who gives a wedding feast for his son (Matt 22:2–13). (3) Yet Jesus also is hailed as king by the multitudes and He does not rebuke them for it (Luke 19:36–40). (4) The disciples believed Jesus was about to enter his kingdom. Jesus does not deny it but counsels that they think in terms of humble service rather than of their status in the kingdom (Matt 20:20–28). (5) Indeed, in some passages of the New Testament there appear to be two kingdoms—a kingdom of the Son and of the Father (Matt 13:36–43; 16:24–28; 25:31–46; Col 1:13–14). How are these two to be reconciled? (6) Similarly, it is not entirely clear whether the Christ is actively to bring enemies into subjection or whether his role is to be passive, of sitting at the Lord's right hand (Matt 22:41–46). (7) For St. Paul the uncertainty is resolved in favor of viewing the present as the age in which the Christ is bringing enemies under subjugation, but at the end He will turn His kingdom back to the Father who has given it (1 Cor 15:24). (8) As long as enemies of hatred, envy and cruelty remain to be subjected, we are living in that interim period when Christ is seeking to establish His kingdom. The preceding inquiry may be summarized: the story of Nebuchadnezzar has thus prefigured the New Testament teaching that the rule and strength and power and majesty of Christ's kingdom reside not in worldly might and self-exaltation, but rather in self-abasement and humble praise of a wondrous God who alone is king above all earthly powers.

## National Destiny and Divine Providence/ The Spirit of the Holy God Is in You (4:4–18)

In these verses Nebuchadnezzar relates his dream, his unsuccessful attempt to find Babylonian interpreters and his reason for confidence in Daniel's ability to come up with the desired interpretation which will both explain, and therefore also remove the threat of, the dream. The dream is clearly political and similar to the dream of chapter two, wherein a destruction of the king's kingdom is also foreshadowed. At least two sermons may be developed on the basis of these verses. The first of these on "National Destiny and Divine Providence" might develop the following points.

(A) The positive benefits of a strong national power are many and may be seen to be but a means of divine providence. (1) In some places in Scripture the nations count as nothing before God (Dan 4:35; Isa 40:17, etc.). (2) The Bible recognizes the demonic dimension, arrogance, and tendencies toward self-deification in national states, and is unmistakable in its harsh reminders of the divine judgment on national pretensions and wilful subjugation of other nations or peoples (Isa 14, 47; Ezek 28; Amos 1—2; Rev 18). (3) In these verses the nation is shown to be but an instrument of divine providence in furnishing for the needs of the people. Some of the benefits explicitly mentioned or clearly indicated are: (a) an abundance of food, (b) protection and shelter (suggested by branches furnishing shade), (c) peace (v. 1), and (d) tranquility (v. 27). (4) The name Nebuchadnezzar means, in Akkadian, "May Nebo (the god) protect the boundary"; the story shows that it is the Most High, not Nebo, who establishes and protects earthly kingdoms.

(B) To what extent is the destiny of a nation in the hands of its own people? In response to this question the Scripture has two dominant views: (1) National destiny is in the hands of God and is determined by the divine counsels (vv. 13–17), and (2) a degree of self-determination is allowed. The divine is affected by the extent of justice and mercy shown to the oppressed (v. 27).

(C) Possible reasons why the divine might decree to wield the axe on our nation. (1) A failure to practice justice and mercy. (2) Placing such a reliance on military power as a means of keeping the peace that other crucial means are neglected: (a) investment of monies in language programs so that more of our people can converse with and know our potential foes rather than treat them simply as instruments of the devil; (b) cultural exchange programs; (c) fostering literacy, self-development and the increase of persons who own their own property. (I recently heard a passionate plea from a former missionary to Latin America that we stop indiscriminate military support there of suppressive and anti-democratic regimes. Instead of missiles, he urged we send missionaries and teachers who will help increase public health, literacy, a sense of human dignity, and the tools for self-development as well as the love of God and commitment to democracy.) (3) See also above on pp. 31–32 the sermon suggestion, "The American Image," section E.

One important clue on what to stress in a sermon may be found by noting what the text itself emphasizes. In 4:4–18,

Nebuchadnezzar underlines three times that it is because the spirit of the holy god is in Daniel that he has confidence in Daniel to furnish an interpretation to this dream (vv. 8, 9, 18). A sermon is clearly in order to explore the meaning of: "The Spirit of the Holy God Is in You." Such a sermon might be developed as follows.

(A) What qualities, attributes, or training cause us to seek out one professional above others? Some suggested answers might include: (1) superior skill and knowledge acquired in home-training and learning prior to advanced education (such as the king sought: 1:3–4); (2) superior advanced education (such as Daniel and his friends received at Nebuchadnezzar's court, 1:5, 20); (3) natural endowments, skills and abilities in discernment (gifts from God) which distinguish one professional from another (1:17); or (4) confidence that the spirit of God is resident in the one sought out (especially in matters that pertain to human relations and spiritual affairs).

(B) How may the presence or absence of the Spirit of God in a professional be discerned? (1) From the point of view of the Old Testament: (a) skill itself is viewed as a divine gift (1:17); (b) the one in whom the Spirit of God resides will have a sense of: (i) joy in living, (ii) health, integrity, and wholeness (Ps 51:11–12: the meaning of "salvation" is closely aligned to that of *shalom*, "peace") which derives, at least in part from (iii) a thorough self-knowlege of sin and of divine forgiveness (Ps 51:1–9, 13–14), and therefore (iv) a degree of genuine, and not unctious, humility (Ps 51:15–17). (2) From the point of view of the New Testament those in whom the spirit resides may be in part at least determined (a) in a negative test, if the individual in question is not: (i) jealous, (ii) boastful, (iii) rude, (iv) insistent on its own way, (v) irritable, (vi) resentful, (vii) joyful over wrong or harm to others (1 Cor 13:4–6), and (b) in a positive test, if the following fruits of the spirit are present: (i) love, (ii) joy, (iii) peace, (iv) patience, (v) kindness, (vi) goodness, (vii) faithfulness, (viii) gentleness, and (ix) self-control.

(C) These qualities may be absent from us in varying degrees, but we may seek them individually and together as a church. (1) Mutual edification (lit. "up-building") is at least one of the reasons for the existence of the church. (Eph 4:1–16 has always been to me a very moving statement of the purpose of Christian fellowship, namely, together to grow up into the measure of the fullness of the stature of Christ.) (2) There is a dialectic on the presence of the spirit: the beginning of the presence of the divine spirit commences with a genuine awareness of: (a) one's own faults and sin (Ps 51) and (b) of one's own weaknesses (Rom 8:26-27, see also 1 Cor 1:25).

## Mental Health/A Sense of the Divine/Angels (4:19-27)

In these verses Daniel at first wishes the interpretation of the dream on the king's enemies (an indication of bad news); he then gives the interpretation which ends on a hopeful note of restoration for the king if he acknowledges the kingship of Yahweh (the good news). Curiously, even though these verses furnish the *peshar*, "interpretation," they tell less about the king's ailment than the dream itself (v. 16) and the fulfillment (vv. 34, 36). The impending disaster turns out to be not only a loss of his kingdom for seven times, i.e. years (vv. 16, 23), but also clearly a mental ailment. Because of this and because an angel is an intermediary for the divine decree (vv. 13, 23) and because a turning point for the king depends upon whether or not he has a sufficient sense of the rule of the Most High, three sermons would seem to be logical developments from these verses. The first of these on "Mental Health" might be shaped as follows.

(A) The subject of mental health is implicit in much of Scripture and occasionally also explicitly dealt with. (1) Examples of the concern of Scripture for mental and emotional well-being are many: (a) the bestowal of peace, blessing, joy and salvation in the Old Testament all include the idea of peace of mind and mental as well as physical wholeness and well-being. (b) A source of such well-being is the praise of God: (i) "Bless the Lord, O my soul, and let all that is within me bless his holy name" points to an inner harmony, an emotional unity, brought about in part through praise. (ii) "Thou shalt love the Lord thy God with all thy heart, with all thy soul and with all thy might" (Deut 6:5) also points in the same direction. (c) One of the most moving examples of how sexual experience can affect mental health is found in the so-called Court History of David: after her seduction and rape by her half-brother, "Tamar dwelt a desolate woman" (2 Sam 13:20). (d) In the New Testament the fruits of the spirit indicate a mental harmony and well-being in contrast to the works of the flesh which show the marks of mental and emotional disharmony (Gal 5:16–24). (2) Even more explicitly: (a) God is not only the author of wisdom, He takes away discernment and understanding from elders and leaders (Job 12:13–25, Dan 4:16) and (b) returns it (Dan 4:34, 36).

(B) From the biblical point of view a preservation and restoration of mental health is dependent therefore on: (1) praise; (2) confession and awareness of forgiveness (Ps 51); (3) acknowledgment of God's kingship (Dan 4:25); and (4) "breaking off of" sins (lit. "missing of the mark") by practicing righteousness, and of iniquities (lit. "perversions") by showing mercy (Greek: "almsgiving") to the oppressed (Dan 4:27).

(C) Is the biblical way too simple—that tranquility and length of days come from acknowledging God and from acts of kindness (v. 27)? Or, is there profound wisdom in pointing to outward, even physical acts as the means to maintain and restore mental health? In response to these questions, consider the following: (1) Part of the wisdom of the Israelite sacrificial system lay in its providing a concrete, visible, even smellable means whereby human beings could acknowledge their sins and the seriousness of them before God. (2) Sacrifices cost the worshiper something and they also involved concrete acts which the penitent sinner had to perform (purchasing of, and bringing, the sacrifice). (3) These seemingly primitive provisions have much to teach us still about the ways that mental health may be attained. (4) Guilt and feelings of guilt unatoned and unforgiven can be tremendously destructive. (5) Symbolic acts of reconciliation and reparation therefore still hold great therapeutic value for one who has offended. (6) We cannot separate altogether responsibilities to, and love of, God from responsibilities to, and love of, our fellow human beings, as Jesus so eloquently put it in Matt 5:23–24. (7) The way to mental and emotional health lies in the fulfillment of both responsibilities.

A second sermon might be developed from these verses on "A Sense of the Divine." It was this "sense" which was decisive for the restoration of the kingdom and of reason to

Nebuchadnezzar. Every pastor should seek to create in the service of worship over which he/she presides an enhanced sense of the divine presence and reality among all worshipers. This can really only be accomplished, as the pastor himself or herself practices the presence through daily prayer and study. If the service is thrown together, the people will know it. If the pastor rushes through life without lifting up his eyes to heaven, the congregation will know it—and be the poorer for it. The previous sermon on mental health is in a sense also a guide for the spiritual well-being of the pastor too. A sermon on "A Sense of God" might go as follows.

(A) A "sense of God" is a gift which any and all of the people of God may rightly desire. (1) The biblical psalmist asks God: "Satisfy us early in the morning with thy mercy" (Ps 90:14), that is, to grant to the petitioner and his companions a sense of the divine presence and forgiveness. (2) One of the functions of worship is to keep alive in times of the divine absence the remembrance of past visitations and manifestations of God (so Samuel Terrien in *The Elusive Presence*).

(B) The God of the Bible is at once: (i) transcendant and immanent, (ii) universal and just, and therefore (iii) holy. Any sense of the divine which lacks these elements will be deficient. (1) The majesty, yet nearness, of God is eloquently presented in Isa 6 and 40 and in Pss 102, 103 and 139. There is a tendency among some religious groups which stress reason and morality to understress the divine glory; others who insist on the divine majesty may deprive themselves and others of the equally important biblical stress on the divine presence (as at the incarnation and in the spirit now). (2) The gods of nationalism and of race may be satisfying to the individual because of their offering the opportunity for commitment to a cause and entity larger than one's self, but these will not in the final analysis be satisfying because they are too narrow and provincial and therefore also less than just. (3) The God of the Bible is throughout portrayed as holy, whose holiness requires: (a) purity of individual actions (the teaching of the wisemen, Ps 25); (b) a purity of right ritual (the teaching of the priests, Lev 19:1–8); (c) a purity of social justice (the teaching of the prophets, Isa 5:16; 6; Amos 5:21–24).

(C) The king in Dan 4 presents a model of one who possesses a sense of the divine. (1) After losing his kingdom and reason for a time, he comes to an awareness, through his suffering, of the divine sovereignty over human affairs (as also in Job 32–37). (2) He learns humility (the counterpart or reverse side of the coin of the above awareness). This newly found insight into the limits of his power includes also a moving out to others in acts of righteousness and giving (see also the example of King Lear). (3) He expresses his new found awareness in praise. Thus, gratitude is part of his sense of God. (A. Solzhenitsyn's novella *One Day in the Life of Ivan Denisovitch* is a beautiful portrayal also of the practical consequences of the theological virtue of gratitude.)

A third sermon based on 4:19–27 might be called "Outlaw Angels?" and might commence with the following introduction. A case could be made that we should no longer make reference to angels in speech or song. If they do not exist, should we not "travel light" and strip away all unnecessary metaphysical baggage? Angels belong to the realm of dispensable romanticism. So why not dispense with all references to them? The body of the sermon might then continue.

(A) In the Bible angels function in three main ways. (1) Angels appear in the Bible as symbols of God's glory, goodwill and desert of praise (angels of presence). (a) Ten thousand are said to have been present at the giving of the law on Mt. Sinai (Deut 33:2; cf. Acts 7:53, Gal 3:19); (b) A multitude was present announcing the birth of Christ (Luke 2:13–14); (c) In the intertestamental period the belief grew up that they were present even at the creation (Jubilees 1:29). (2) Angels appear in the Bible as symbols of the divine desire to protect and minister to humankind who are faithful to Him (guardian angels). (a) The righteous man, Lot, is warned to flee for his life from the cities on which the divine judgment is about to fall (Gen 19); (b) Similarly, angels protect, and minister to, the refugees Hagar (Gen 16) and Elijah (1 Kings 19), and Moses (Exod 3:1–12) and Jesus (Matt 4:1–11) in the wilderness. (c) Even in military matters an angel is sent before Israel to fight for them (Josh 5:13–15; see also the refrain of the hymn, "Onward Christian Soldiers"). (d) Closely related to this is the idea that each nation is granted an angel to protect it (Dan 10; Ps 82; Deut 32:8). (e) Some natural phenomena such as storms with accompanying rain and lightning are viewed as angels and ministers of God (Pss 104:1–4; 29). (3) Angels also appear in the Bible as symbols of the divine judgment (angels of wrath and watchers). Some natural phenomena (wind, storm, disease) which may be instruments of God's judgment (Pss 8:7–19; 46) are also viewed as angels (Ps 104:4; Rev 7:1, 2; 16:1–11).

(B) In the Bible some of the tasks performed by angels are also performed by human beings. (1) Angels are messengers—sometimes warning (as with Lot) or bringing words of impending judgment (as with Nebuchadnezzar in Dan 4). (a) In some instances the angels in question may have been humans (Gen 18). (b) In other instances the functions of angels are performed by human beings. (i) Ezekiel is called to be a watchman and warner (Ezek 33:1–6); (ii) the prophets generally in the Old Testament are messengers of the divine announcing impending judgment, calling to repentance, or bearing glad tidings of coming salvation; (iii) the last book in the English Old Testament, Malachi, the name of a prophet, means "my messenger." (2) Human beings are also chosen to be comforters and pastors to the people in time of need: the prophets Jeremiah, Ezekiel, and Isaiah of Babylon are outstanding examples.

(C) Should angels be outlawed? (1) Some people say that it is deceptive and untrue to allow young children to believe in Santa Claus when he doesn't exist. Should the same thing apply to angels? (2) Christmas without angels? Our lives would be impoverished, our religious imaginations stultified, and our conception of God rendered more bland if angels were stricken from the biblical record and mention of them prohibited. (3) Some recent theologicans seriously argue for the ontological status (real existence) of angels (Karl Barth, James Macquarrie, Billy Graham). (4) Whether or not one concludes angels exist or are important religious symbols, there is a sense in which all persons are called of God to be angels: messengers of His grace, agents of comfort, instruments of protection. (The face of Stephen giving testimony to his faith before the synagogue, became as the face of an angel, Acts 6:15.) (5) Yes, Virginia, there are angels (paraphrasing the famous response of the editor of a former New York evening newspaper to a young girl when she inquired in a letter: "Does Santa exist?").

## Words at the End of the Road (4:34–37)

In terms of subject matter these verses belong together with vv. 1–3. The last verse fittingly summarizes the teaching of the chapter. A sermon might be preached on this verse, with the three main parts providing the structure of the sermon outline, starting with the last part first. Such a sermon entitled "Words at the End of the Road" might have as an introduction the following. A dominant metaphor of life in the Bible is that of walking (Pss 23:4; 119:105; 143:8–9; Micah 6:6). In 4:37 we have the last words of the royal figure who features in the first four chapters of the book. To what extent do these words supply a model for what we might wish to say at the end of our road? The main points of the sermon might then be: (A) Have we learned humility in the walk of our life? (see above pp. 47–49). (B) Have we come to the conviction that the works of God are reliable and his ways just? (C) Has praise become a way of life? (see above   p. 27). (D) If none of the above, what are your alternatives?

## Sic Transit Gloria/Holy Seasons/The Hand of God/ Dilemmas/Sons and Fathers (5:1–23)

One of the most fabulous banquets of modern times was given in October 1971. "Under a ceiling of shimmering silk, the 600 guests sat down to a five-hour banquet that began with . . . quail eggs stuffed with caviar. The main course was roast peacock served in its own brilliant plumage." The *Life Magazine* report continues, "For four fabulous days and nights, 160 acres of desert near Iran's ancient ruins of Persepolis came alive in a glittering tribute to a nation's past. It was the 2500th anniversary of the founding of the Persian empire, and Shah Reza Pahlavi had invited the world's leaders to celebrate. They came from 69 nations: one emperor, eight kings and a cardinal, grand dukes, crown princes and sheiks, presidents, premiers and vice presidents, including Spiro and Mrs. Agnew of the United States. They dined sumptuously . . . and drank the finest wine." Before the 1970's were over, the Shah was forced to flee from the country he once ruled with grandeur. Less than ten years after the fabulous banquet, the Shah was dead (July 27, 1980). The banquet and the demise of the Shah in exile is a modern commentary on Dan 5 and the ephemerality of worldly glory.

This chapter offers the preacher the opportunity to reflect on: the function of celebrations (v. 1), profanation of the sacred (vv. 2–9), solving life's riddles (vv. 10–23) and on a specific biblical anagram (vv. 24–31). Instead of supplying suggested sermon outlines as in the previous chapters, some comments will be made on these groups of verses.

A sermon could be built around the first verse, using the example of the Shah of Iran as a contemporary illustration, but more particularly developing the idea of sacred times and seasons. There is a time and a place for celebration, for looking back, and for emphasizing particular values and traditions of the Judeo-Christian heritage. Jewish-Christian congregations remember and celebrate Passover along with Good Friday, the Festival of Weeks along with Pentecost, the Feast of the Ninth of Ab (of the Fall of Jerusalem), New Year (Rosh Hashanah), the Day of Atonement (Yom Kippur), Tabernacles (Succoth), and Joy of the Torah (Simchath Torah). It would be strained perhaps for predominantly Gentile congregations to enrich their Christian remembrances by specific celebration of ancient Israelite and modern Jewish holy days. It would not be out of place in a sermon, however, to note the particular emphases of Israelite-Jewish holy days. A little study and note-taking in any good dictionary of the Bible or of Judaica will be rewarding.

In vv. 2–9 a prime example is given of a profanation of the sacred: the vessels of the temple are desecrated. Here again, the sermon need not focus on the negative, but could reflect upon what it is that makes a thing or a place holy and set apart. The severed hand which features in these verses brings a negative message of judgment. A sermon on the "Hand of God" need not be one of doom. The hand and finger of God are powerful biblical metaphors for the divine presence, strength, providence, and comfort. Using a concordance will quickly reveal the rich possibilities for this subject.

Verses 10–23 present the solution to the threatening, enigmatic message of the handwriting on the wall. The threat is not removed, but it is interpreted and clarified. The preacher may thus choose to list several kinds of contemporary dilemmas: financial, marital, familial and suggest at least some solutions—drawing on his/her pastoral experiences, the Scripture, the wisdom of modern counsellors, and the social sciences. In such a sermon the pastor may choose to address himself/herself to recurring problems in the parish. An esteemed rabbi in my part of the country recently preached on Yom Kippur a no-holds-barred sermon on divorce. Some of the congregation, and not only the singles, were upset. The rabbi's pastoral and prophetic insight struck where it hurt.

Verses 10–23 draw the contrast between father and son. A sermon to the fathers (on allowing the sons room for individuality and freedom of vocational choice) and to the sons (on the meaning of respect) would be in order. Or, a sermon on the limits beyond which one should not press a comparison between father and son, mother and daughter!

## A Biblical Anagram/Determinism and Free-Will/ The Handwriting on the Wall (5:24–31)

The biblical writers delighted in puns. At least three puns underlie the moving hand. (i) *Mene, tekel* and *parsin* are participles which mean "numbered," "weighed," and "divided." God appears as a merchant or judge. (ii) The participles are also the names of weights, possibly meant to be an evaluation of four kings. The first two, *minas*, are heavy and of great worth. The third, *shekel*, is one fiftieth of a *mina*. The fourth, a *peres* is half a *mina*, or possibly half a *shekel*. *Parsin* is a plural (and possibly dual) form and means "two half-minas." (iii) *Parsin* also meant "Persian." "The theological significance of the passage lies ... on the surface, however interesting the solution of the philological puzzle may be." (Norman Porteous). God has *numbered* the days of the kingdom of the Babylonian monarch Belshazzar and has brought it to an end; he has been *weighed* in the balance and found wanting; his kingdom is about to be *divided* and given to the Medes and Persians. Destiny is divinely determined.

A sermon would be in order in which the preacher explores the topic of "Determinism and Free-Will." It might be developed along these lines. (A) There are forms of social determinism. (Human behavior is greatly affected by environment.) (B) There are forms of psychological determinism.

(Genetic make-up may affect the nature of human actions
more than rearing and social environment.) (C) In the divine
determinism, human freedom is given a large role; neither
genetic make-up nor social milieu are so strong they cannot
at least in part be altered. In the divine determinism, human
action calls forth certain kinds of response—not always de-
terminable, but predictable within limits and yet laden with
surprises. God is as the great chess master. (D) The social sciences and belief in divine providence and determinism are
not at odds. Neither are the social sciences a substitute for a
study of Scripture and history in order to discern the patterns of the divine dialogue with humankind.

Another sermon, "The Handwriting on the Wall" might be
developed out of these verses. So deeply has this chapter entered into Western consciousness the expression "handwriting
on the wall" is widely understood to mean "clear indications
that a calamity is about to strike." What handwriting do we
discern on the walls of our suburban and extra-urban ghettos?
Does the prevalence of the uplifted hand of the mugger tell us
something of a divine weighing of our society in the balances?
Have we been found wanting? Do we need a contemporary
Daniel to interpret? Such a sermon could be developed along
three different lines: (i) exploring the whole science of futurolo-
gy, describing it, commending it, but calling for an inclusion of
the theological dimension; (ii) discussing the popular fad of
reading the Bible as a gypsy reads a crystal ball (to determine
the events of the present and future); (iii) emphasizing the need
for social action and consciences awakened to human suffering
in the inner cities, the graffiti of which we would rather not
read. Under (iii) one could discuss the immensely popular
books, *The Late Great Planet Earth*, and *Satan is Now Alive and
Well* by Hal Lindsey (on whom see a review under 7:1–8). I was
greatly helped to reach some historical perspective on the
American form of dispensational thinking by reading Ernest
Sandeen's fine study, *The Roots of Fundamentalism*. Conservative Protestants and Catholics with dispensationalist leanings
may be surprised at the extent to which the Scofield Reference
Bible and the tendency to read the Bible as a predictive device
has roots in the teaching of the Plymouth Brethren of the nine-
teenth century and in the teachings of John Nelson Darby in
particular.

# Faith's Response
# to the Legal Crunch
## (Daniel 6:1–28)

In many eyes the high water mark of the book of Daniel is chapter six. The story is so well-known it is astonishing how many things new the scribes trained for the kingdom have brought forth out of this treasure. Four items in particular have been established within the past decades of scholarship.

First, it has been shown that the chapter "incorporates" sentences such as the following from Ps 57:4–6: "I lie in the midst of lions that greedily devour the sons of men; their teeth are spears and arrows, their tongues sharp swords. Be exalted, O God, above the heavens! Let Thy glory be over all the earth! They set a net for my steps; my soul was bowed down. They dug a pit in my way, but they have fallen into it themselves." Second, this chapter has been classified as a tale of court contest—calling attention to the conflict between the Median and Persian courtiers who are so envious of Daniel they seek to lay a legal trap for him, to do him in. Third, it has been shown that Daniel functions here (as the three friends do also in chapter three) as a "light to the Gentiles," that is, as a model of conduct and piety so devout that the pagan king acknowledges Yahweh's sovereignty and His power to save (see Isa 42:6; 49:6). Fourth, modern scholarship has called our attention again to an obvious, but easily overlooked, aspect of the text, namely, how much the focus of attention turns upon the secular law of ordinances, interdicts, and decrees, and in turn, how these may be used for religious suppression or toleration.

## Character/The Law as a Weapon/ Daniel and Joseph/Daniel and Jesus (6:1–9)

Daniel receives honor and status, and the Median courtiers are envious. Daniel's character is such that they can find no fault in his conduct or performance of duty, so they decide to use the law as a club with which to beat him down. They will trap him on the basis of his character and religion. Their schemings, however, do not exactly have the desired outcome. They are successful in manipulating the king and the laws to their own advantage. The king signs an edict which prohibits religious devotion to any other save to the king himself. Daniel seems doomed.

Four sermons may be developed from these verses. One on "Character" might take as its text: "They could find no ground for complaint nor any fault, because he was faithful, and no error or fault was found in him" (RSV: v. 4; see also NEB). This sermon could explore the notion of, and forces that foster, character. Key New Testament texts are Rom 5:1–5 and Heb 1:3. The sermon might start with a story of a "character," i.e., an unusual person whom you know. The preacher then could move from the "character" as unusual and unforgettable person to personal character, that is, "character" which means "moral integrity" or "the presence in a person of a high degree of virtue so that a pattern of upright conduct in relation to fellow human beings may almost invariably be counted upon." Several different examples of persons possessed of character could be given. Immanuel Kant, the philosopher, was so regular in his habits of study and daily walks that it was said people could set their watches by him. Harry Truman would not use public funds for personal letters—not even for a three cent stamp! When the Nazis ordered Jews to wear a yellow arm band, the King of Denmark appeared wearing a yellow arm band, and the whole nation followed suit. When Albert Einstein learned the Germans did not have the atomic bomb, he labored hard to block the plan of the United States to use it. A second section could explore how suffering adversity produces endurance and endurance character (Rom 5:1–5). A third section could then explore what difference it would make to the nation if instead of the upbuilding of character and decency, an egoistical ethic were substituted.

This chapter displays a keen awareness of how secular laws may affect human conduct. A sermon on May Day or United Nations Day (October 24) or upon the installation or death of a supreme court justice, would be an appropriate occasion for a sermon on this chapter and the function of law. A conversation with some of the attorneys in the congregation might also be useful in gaining insights into the philosophy of law and into some of the problems faced by attorneys. One of my teachers, Reinhold Niebuhr, used to stress that the only way the commandment of love will be put into effect in a technological society is not simply to perform acts of kindness toward individuals, but to seek to establish justice by affecting the structures of society through legal means. In this task of caring and laboring to put into effect the commandment of love by striving for just legislation, church people must not grow weary. Dan 6 shows a sophisticated awareness of how laws can be used to punish certain people for their religious persuasion and practices. The Nazis started early on their path toward genocide by passing laws adverse to Jews. South Africa uses its laws to deny the right of private ownership to blacks. In this country the requirement for persons to pass a literacy test and to be taxpayers before they could vote was, for a long time, used to disenfranchise many blacks. Christians who really take the Bible and its teachings of love and justice seriously have a solemn obligation to work for more just and humane laws at home and abroad. A sermon on law could call attention to (i) the relationship between the commandment of love and working toward justice through laws; (ii) even in a democracy the mere ability to muster a majority vote on any issue does not give the majority in the sight of God any moral right to punish members of different religious or ethnic groups, or callously to overlook the handicaps that poverty and years of past exploitation have placed especially heavily on racial and ethnic minorities; and (iii) the necessity for constant vigilance, intelligent surveillance of the impact of legislation and a willingness to work for changes of laws when unforeseen injustices or unfairnesses become apparent.

A third or fourth sermon based on these verses could contrast Daniel and Joseph (Gen 37—50) and Daniel and Jesus. The main point in the third sermon would be to show how even human evil God may turn to good (Gen 50:20). The main point in the fourth sermon would be to show that even though a number of parallels can be cited between Jesus and Daniel, Jesus for the Christian was more than a morally upright man of high character. We may seek to emulate the character of both and we may try the harder to emulate the character of Jesus because it was morally so sublime, but we should not naively (and arrogantly!) expect that we will ever attain the measure of the stature of the fullness of Jesus the Christ, even though we might possibly attain the stature of Daniel. The pastor will want to draw up his/her own list of parallels. Here are a few points of similarity between Daniel and Joseph.

(A) Daniel and Joseph on the face of it had a number of similar external events transpire in their careers: both ended up in a foreign land, serving in the court of an overlord or king in an official capacity; both were skilled in the interpretation of dreams; both learned the language of the overlord; both were pressed to be unfaithful to the religious law of their fathers and mothers (Daniel to violate the food laws and to cease in prayer; and Joseph to commit adultery); both were imprisoned for refusing to reject the precepts of the religious law they had inherited and appropriated; for both the apparent moment of being cast in confinement of pit or prison became the occasion for an ultimate deliverance and elevation.

(B) Daniel and Joseph also displayed similar responses to their largely pagan environment: both displayed a superior skill and wisdom, excelling their peers and pagan counterparts; both remained faithful to the faith in which they were raised; both displayed moral integrity, courage, and a fear of God.

(C) The theological outcome for these two was also similar. In both instances (of Joseph's suffering evil at the hands of his brothers and Daniel's near suffering of death because of scheming and envious courtiers) the divine sovereignty is seen to be at work. (i) In Daniel's case fidelity leads not only to advancement but to the pagan king's acknowledgment of God's power and to the king's issuance of an edict of toleration; (ii) in Joseph's case, God uses the evil intent of the brothers to work an ultimate good (the preservation of life of many, including the sons of Israel, in time of severe famine). (iii) Both of these examples of the divine using of faithfulness and suffering for an ultimate good may be seen as examples or patterns of the divine working in history which are repeated, albeit in a new degree of intensity, in the faithfulness and suffering of Jesus at the hands of humans who wished him ill.

A sermon on Daniel and Jesus might show that even though there are many similarities between Jesus and heroes of the Old Testament such as Daniel, there are differences too which underline how and why for the Christian Jesus is more than a good man of heroic proportions.

(A) There are similarities between Daniel and Jesus. Both were steadfast in prayer. Both were nurtured in the tradition of the Torah and upheld by word and practice its importance. Even though the official responsible for putting into effect the death penalty expressed reluctance in so doing with respect to both, a decision was reached within an imperially accepted judicial process that each had committed an offense which legally warranted the death penalty. Both were delivered from the instruments of capital punishment: Daniel through a divine deliverance and closing of the lion's mouths; Jesus through resurrection from the dead after death.

(B) There are a number of significant points of contact between the Narrative of Daniel and the Gospel Narrative. In both Daniel (4:31) and the Gospels (Matt 3:13–17; Mark 9:7) a "voice from heaven" is heard. Angelic intermediaries feature in both, one of whom (Gabriel), bears the same name (Dan 9:20–23; Luke 1:26–31). A belief in the resurrection from the dead, which in Dan 12:1–3 is expressed as an article of faith, in the Gospels is given a full expression as a divinely accomplished act in Jesus (Matt 28; Mark 16; Luke 24; John 20—21). In the book of Daniel the "Son of Man" is a key figure whose coming in the clouds and receipt of the kingdom are viewed in many of the Gospel texts as prophecies which were fulfilled in Jesus (Matt 11:3; 20:18; 25:31; Mark 8:31—9:13). (For further treatment see also the next chapter.)

(C) Differences between Daniel and Jesus are nonetheless considerable. Jesus did not serve as a courtier in a foreign, royal court, but served rather as an itinerant preacher chiefly, but not exclusively, among circles outside the imperial court. Jesus did not gain a reputation for the successful interpretation of dreams but for his teaching on the kingdom and his healing. Stories of deliverance from death are told of both, but of Daniel it was not affirmed that his suffering and death were atoning, healing and creative of a restored relationship between God and humankind. Jesus thus has heroic proportions, as does Daniel, but neither a crucifixion nor a resurrection of Daniel are proclaimed to have taken place, nor was Daniel's suffering salvific as is the case with Jesus.

## The Risks of Commitment/Prayer/*In Extremis:* Civil Disobedience (6:10–18)

Despite his clear knowledge that the proposed interdict has been put into law, Daniel returns to the upper room of his home, falls down on his knees and prays to God thrice daily. He risks his life—for prayer! The jealous courtiers burst into his chamber, catch him in the act of civil disobedience, and report him forthwith to the king. (For more on King Darius, see my comments below on 9:1–2.) The friendly king seeks to find a loophole in the legalities of the interdict, is unsuccessful in so doing, and then personally seals Daniel in the pit of lions with a benedictory prayer: "May your God whom you serve continually, deliver you!" Once back at the palace he fasts, abstains from all pleasures and undergoes a sleepless night— wondering, no doubt, what will become of Daniel.

Three sermons might be developed from these verses. In "The Risks of Commitment," the preacher would examine: (A) Important Human Commitments; (B) The Meaning and Effect of Commitment to God, and (C) The Risks of Human and Theological Commitment—and non-Commitment!

(A) List the range of human commitments and choose to explore only one or two: (1) friendship (which may be for a few months, years, or a lifetime); (2) marriage (which hopefully and ideally will be for a lifetime); (3) family (paternity and maternity carry concomitant responsibilities for nurture, emotional and psychological support of offspring); (4) allegiance to nation (in time of war may call for an ultimate commitment); (5) loyalty to business or firm (may require a commitment of time which will overshadow other commitments); (6) avocations, hobbies; (7) clubs; (8) volunteer service. A philosophy of stewardship of time is clearly needed. (How does one order the diverse demands on time and energies? Merely punching the clock and physical presence alone is no substitute for an undivided and self-giving presence with spouse, family, or God!)

(B) Explore the effect of commitment to God on other commitments. (1) A profound commitment to God will put other commitments in perspective and aid in the setting of priorities. (2) Prayer (creative meditation, thanksgiving, and intercession) may be seen not simply as a luxury—a dispensible item—but as an essential for full and creative living wherein one is enabled to give the most of himself or herself to others. (3) To make one's highest commitment to any person, institution or idea (even an idea of God!) will be idolatry and will almost invariably lead to some form of distress—such, in any event, is the clear message of the Bible.

(C) Commitment means risk, yet remaining non-commital may mean death. (1) Without commitment one will remain in infancy. (2) Lifelong commitments bear with them risks of hurt, suffering, pain, and anguish (if the ones to whom commitments are made disappoint, die, or should fail us in some way). (3) To refrain from making commitments is one way of excluding and minimizing pain—and also joy! (4) To refrain from theological commitment may be a form of self-willed confinement to infancy or adolescence. (5) As is the case in the natural world, a goal in life is growth, flowering, and bearing fruit. (6) Such a flowering and fullness is nurtured by theological commitment. Life is commitment.

A sermon on "Prayer" should be the product of mature reflection and practice. The pastor who has not made regular (preferably daily) prayer a practice should probably pass on this subject. The congregation will uncannily sense if a pastor is once removed from his/her subject. On the other hand, even a whisper and a stammer from a man or woman of prayer will have a considerable impact. These verses speak of the place of prayer (an upper room, i.e., a place apart from the immediate intrusion of persons from the street), the frequency of prayer (often!), the kinds of prayer (thanksgiving, petition, supplication). The classics of Oswald Chambers, William Law, Friedrich Heiler, George A. Buttrick, Henri Nouwen, and the Psalms have been helpful to me. The first congregation I served enjoyed greatly a series of adult studies in which we read and discussed Buttrick's *Prayer*. In good preaching, however, there is no substitute for the personal word. Let the organization come from your own experience, guided also by the structure of the text. Two of the many messages of the sermon might be: (i) prayer is a means of grace; (ii) Daniel risked his physical life to remain constant in prayer because he was certain that life without prayer would soon have become a form of death. (For further thoughts on prayer, and especially the role of confession and the putting away of self-righteousness, see below on 9:3–20.)

A third sermon on these verses might be devoted to the subject of civil disobedience. By the Latin phrase *in extremis* ("in dire straits"), I mean, Daniel does not take to civil disobedience lightly. The lawyer and theologian John Calvin in his commentary on Daniel defends civil disobedience *if* the laws disobeyed are contrary to the law of God. Citizens must of necessity be exceedingly cautious in glibly assigning the label "contrary to the law of God" to any ordinance which causes inconvenience or conflicts with self-interest. The former diplomat to Russia, George Kennan, eloquently reminded us during the 60's of how many atrocities in history have been committed by persons who were convinced they were on the side of the angels and of God. The message of these verses is that ordinances are to be followed unless the situation is *in extremis*, in radical violation of divine law. An overly easy violation of law for selfish ends may easily backfire, and end in having a corrosive effect on the integrity of government and on citizen respect for law. The alert pastor will find, alas, many examples at hand. By way of caution, especially to younger pastors: sit on this sermon and *weigh carefully* whatever contemporary examples you choose before you preach it. It might be helpful and instructive to seek out the counsel of some of the attorneys in the congregation after you have devoted some thought to the subject yourself. Mohandas K. Gandhi's very moving *Autobiography* and Henry Thoreau's essay "Civil Disobedience" and Martin Luther King's "Letter from a Birmingham Jail" are classics on the subject, any one of which the preacher may consult with profit.

## Miraculous Deliverance/Retribution/ Religious Toleration (6:19–28)

The theme of these verses, God's wondrous deliverance of Daniel, is the theme also of Dan 3 and 4:1–3, 34–37. The comments above on these passages may provide some supplementary suggestions suitable for sermons based on 6:19–28.

Retribution is one of the great themes of the Bible. Friedrich Schleiermacher, the renowned theologian of the last century, taught that there were two main doctrines in the Old Testament: the doctrines of election and of retribution. That judgment I take to be an oversimplification but it does serve to underline the prominence in both testaments of the idea: "With what measure ye mete, it shall be meted also unto you" (Matt 7:2). The idea is, in one way, extremely anthropocentric, that is, it makes human action the most important determining point in how a person shall fare in life, and in death. ("And the dead were judged by what was written in the books, by what they had done": Rev 20:12.) This idea is found in classic form in Pss 7:14–16 and 18:25–27. Some of the extreme anthropocentricity of this idea is taken away in the book of Deuteronomy. How human beings fare in life is made more theocentric: hence God may send suffering not because of human sin, but to *test* Israel to see if she would keep the commandments (Deut 8:2), or God may let Israel hunger to *teach* her (Deut 8:3, 5), or God may choose to grant Israel favor *not* because of her righteousness (Deut 9:4–6), but because she is a "peculiar people" (i.e., especially precious) to him (Deut 7:6–7). Despite these obvious reactions against a strict tit for tat and anthropocentric view of retribution, scholars persist in speaking (wrongly!) of the "Deuteronomic view of retribution." Dan 6 expresses in story form the anthropocentric side of the biblical coin of retribution: Daniel's faithfulness is rewarded by the living God's saving him from the power of the lions (6:26–27); *and*, the envious courtiers (and their families) who sought Daniel's harm are punished with the very penalty they had engineered in order to "get" Daniel. A sermon based on these verses could explore the central idea: "Is There Such A Thing As 'Getting Away With It'?" Is life as rewarding as it was to Daniel, and as harsh to the malicious as it was to the envious courtiers? There are two sides to the coin of the biblical view on retribution: (1) human actions count (God does tend, as a rule, but not always, to send rewards and punishments commensurate to human actions), and (2) individual human beings do not have the final or ultimate word in the determination of their own fate in life or death (the final word is God's). See also Prov 16:9; 19:21.

One of the persistent and perplexing issues confronting theists in the Judeo-Christian tradition is: what should our attitude and stance be to other religions? Is the grace of God entirely absent from other faiths? Hans Küng in his moving book *On Being a Christian* assumes a sympathetic stance to world religions and rightly argues that any twentieth-century apologete cannot ignore them. John Macquarrie of Oxford wrestles with this issue and concludes in his *Principles of Christian Theology* that we may discern the operation of divine grace in other religions. In short, the operation of God cannot be confined to our provincial, church box. My experience as an undergraduate teacher of religion causes me to concur wholeheartedly: Christian apologetics will be effective in direct proportion to the sensitivity of the apologete to ennobling and life-nurturing forces in other religions. This does not mean that one must ignore glaring defects in other religions or our own. Rather it means: forceful and effective apologetics in behalf of the Judeo-Christian tradition must come out of an appreciation of the *best* in other traditions and not simply out of a fixation on the crass, the base, and the more obviously deficient. Darius the king in Dan 6 displays a remarkable toleration of the Judaic faith. This passage could thus serve as a suitable spring-board from which the preacher might approach the subject of toleration toward and appreciation of other faiths.

# Beyond the Bestial
## (Daniel 7:1-28)

Chapter seven is pivotal. It brings to an end the Aramaic section (2:4b–7:28) and at the same time introduces the successive visions of 7–12. Like chapters 2, 4 and 5, it contains a symbolic revelation which requires unraveling. It is especially close to chapter two with its succession of four earthly kingdoms, followed by another. There is widespread agreement among recent interpreters that the heavenly imagery in vv. 9–10 and 12–13 draws heavily upon the mythology of ancient Ugarit, that the fifth kingdom is to be contrasted with the beast-like, earthly kingdoms, that the chapter foretells an end to the oppressive power of the fourth beast, and that this chapter has made an important contribution to the New Testament in its portrayal of the Son of Man coming with the clouds. On the other hand, there is sharp disagreement among scholars on the composition of the chapter, the identification of the "One Like a Son of Man" (v. 13), the identification of the "saints of the Most High" (vv. 18, 21, 22, 25 and 27) and even of the "people of the saints of the Most High" (v. 27). Competent scholars maintain the unity of the chapter while others equally as competent see clear signs of supplementation. Some able scholars view the Son of Man as a symbol of the people Israel whereas others, equally as able, see this figure as a heavenly being, an angel—probably Michael. Similarly some argue persuasively that the "saints" are angels while others argue equally as persuasively they are the faithful Israelites. Some even argue that the "people" in v. 27 should properly be rendered "host" and that the expression "people of the saints of the Most High" is a hendiadys (expression of a single thought or idea in two parts) meaning angels rather than Israelites. The preacher should be alert to these divergencies but also aware that they may not be as far apart as even their perpetrators think. For example, if the original author did conceive the "One Like a Son of Man" to be the angelic figure, Michael, the transference of dominion, glory and kingdom to him (v. 13) would constitute also a transferal of the same to Israel below on earth because, as is widely recognized, Michael is Israel's representative. His victories in heaven mean victories for Israel on earth (see 10:13–14, 20–21).

## A New Agenda/Beyond the Crystal Ball/ The Parade of Beasts (7:1–8)

Daniel's first dream vision transpires in the reign of a king (Belshazzar), whose demise, we know from chapter 5, has already come to pass. The name is historically accurate as conservative scholars have pointed out. The eldest son of Nabonidus, Bel-sur-usur, was in all probability the *de facto* ruler in Babylonia while his father Nabonidus was off in the desert at Tema. The setting of the dream is thus during the reign of a king whose soul was suddenly required of him after a night of feasting.

Scholars are in wide agreement that the lion is Babylon; the bear, the Median Empire; the leopard, Persia; and the fourth beast, the Greeks. Chapter eight bears out this identification (8:20–21). John Calvin in his commentary on Daniel makes a passably good defense for the identification of the fourth beast with Rome. The advantage of this identification from the point of view of Christian apologetics is that the interpreter may relate "the anointed one . . . cut off" in 9:26 to the crucifixion of Jesus. The disadvantage is that the weight of internal evidence does not support it as the intention of the original author. A straightforward and honest Christian apologetics which takes biblical scholarship seriously thus on occasion (as on this one) finds itself deprived of some of the arguments used by our forebears to demonstrate the messiahship of Jesus or the great appeal of Christianity. Biblical scholarship urges a rethinking of old defenses. Biblical scholarship is thus threatening to the old orthodoxies and painful for the new orthodoxies which must think through afresh some arguments felt for centuries to be valid. Such a rethinking is a major challenge before the churches for the remaining decades in this century.

Hal Lindsey was not all wrong. In the best-selling *The Late, Great Planet Earth*, Lindsey saw in Dan 7 a prediction of events that would take place in the early 1980's. He even sees in this chapter a foretelling of the European Common Market and of Russian aggression in the Middle East. He has some maps to show how it all will be! It is easy, but perhaps not wise, to scoff rudely at such predictions. I personally do not believe Lindsey's approach to the Bible is correct. (He sees the Bible as a crystal ball which predicts events in our lifetime.) On the other hand, there is a measure of truth which underlies Lindsey's semi-magical understanding of the Bible: that is, the *pattern* of events described in the Bible has (sadly!) a way of repeating itself in successive ages. Nations, alas, still resort to warfare, violence, and bestial conduct. An unspeakable persecution of the saints, that is, persons dedicated to the Most High, has taken place in our own generation by one who makes, in comparison, the persecutions of Antiochus IV Epiphanes seem mild. A second part of the affirmation of Hal Lindsey all theists in the Judeo-Christian tradition can also affirm wholeheartedly, namely, there is an ultimate limit to the evil a demonic foe can work; the divine dominion alone will endure; earthly kingdoms are continually subject to divine judgment and those built upon violence and injustice will not endure. Christian and Jew alike believe that the kingdom of God alone is from generation to generation (Ps 102:11–12, 23–24). For Christians the dominion, which is Christ's for a time, He will return in the end to the Father when all enemies have been subjected under his feet (1 Cor 15:24–28). Misguided though the crystal ball approach to the Scriptures may be, some of its theological insights remain profound and true.

A sermon on these verses might address itself directly to the challenge of biblical studies to apologetics, or it could seek to point out the strengths as well as the weaknesses in the crystal ball approach of Hal Lindsey, or it might develop the idea of acknowledging the beast within individuals and nations which continually requires to be subjected and tamed. A sermon along the latter line might be labelled "The Parade of Beasts" and be developed as follows.

(A) Since the days of early Israel, animals have been selected as emblems and symbols of class and tribes. (1) Gen 49, the Blessing of Jacob, furnishes examples: Judah (the lion), Issachar (bony ass), Dan (serpent), Naphtali (deer), Benjamin (wolf). (2) Anthropological studies of totems and tribal mythology show that a similar practice obtains all over the world. (3) Similarly athletic teams select animal names and mascots to reflect prowess, agility and regional pride (dolphins, bears, cubs, cougars, falcons, razor-back hogs, wild cats). (4) Modern nations follow suit: the eagle (U.S.A.), John Bull (Britain), the bear (Russia), fox (France), elephant or cobra (India), kangaroo (Australia), springbok (South Africa), crocodile (Egypt). (5) Recognition of the long-standing and widespread use of animal symbolism in religion, anthropology and athletics may take something of the strangeness away from the animal symbolism in apocalyptic: lion (Babylonia), bear (Media), leopard (Persia), fourth beast (Greece), horns (individual kings), the "little horn" (Antiochus IV Epiphanes). (See also Dan 8 where the two horns of the ram are the kings of Media and Persia and the first great horn of the he-goat is Alexander the Great, vv. 20–21.) (6) Once the key is found, history can be told quite simply using symbols.

(B) Animals may also serve to exemplify specific individual human traits as well as corporate characteristics. Thus the following common expressions connote the trait in parentheses: (1) "ferocious as a lion," "harmless as a dove" (rapacity/peacefulness); (2) "wise as an owl, serpent," "clever as a fox," "sly as a cat" (sagacity); (3) "clumsy as an ox" (lack of agility); (4) "stubborn as a mule," "to be dogged" (obstinacy/persistence); (5) "faithful as a dog" (loyalty); (6) "eager beaver," "busy as a beaver," "to be a tiger," "lazy as a dog" (activity, vitality, sloth); (7) "messy as a pig," "to be a pig" (untidiness); (8) "to be a snake in the grass" (deceitfulness); (9) "to be lionhearted," "to be chicken" (bravery/cowardice); (10) "to be a wolf," "to act like a rabbit" (sexual activity) (11) "quick as a rabbit," "swift as a greyhound" (alacrity); (12) "to be an ox," "to wolf down food" (lack of gentility); (13) "to monkey around" (lack of seriousness); (14) "to be a skunk, a rat" (questionable moral performance); (15) "to be a dove, a hawk" (peacefulness/bellicosity).

(C) There is a beast within us of different sorts. (1) Perhaps we are like the faint-hearted lion in *The Wizard of Oz*, chicken-livered, cowardly, and need help in overcoming fears and phobias. (2) Perhaps the competitive instinct is so strong we need to tame the tiger, curb its rapacity. (3) Perhaps we give up too soon, play dead like the possum and need to attain a greater self-confidence. (4) The anti-hero in Samuel Butler's *Way of All Flesh* pays a visit to the zoo to soothe his troubled nerves. There is something therapeutic about a trip to the zoo—to gain perspective on ourselves, to help us see some of our comic antics as well as our bestiality. (5) In the book of Job the idea is put forth that animals may instruct us (Job 12:7–12) and in the speeches of God (Job 38–41) in response to Job's question as to why he suffers, God points to His creation of different animals to enable Job to get some perspective on his life and to learn from their ways. (6) The question is: what kind of an animal does God want you to become? (For another conclusion, see also below the suggested sermon under vv. 13–18, item D 5.)

## The Ancient of Days (7:9–12)

In vv. 9–10 the scene shifts to heaven and back in vv. 11–12 again to earth. In heaven Daniel sees thrones and the Ancient of Days, God, takes his seat upon one. The court sits in judgment and the books are opened. This heavenly scene marks the finish of the fourth beast and its boastful horn. Heavenly judgment has immediate effect.

What is interesting about these verses is the utilization of traditional symbolism. The sovereignty of God, the purity of God, the wisdom of God, the majesty of God, and the judgment of God are all portrayed here in ancient, anthropomorphic, and almost crass, symbols. The symbols are as basic as they are simple and child-like. The divine rule is indicated by His throne and by the ten thousands standing before Him; the divine wisdom by the title "Ancient of Days" and by His white hair; the divine purity by His white raiment; the divine majesty by the thousand servants; and the divine judgment by the throne of fire, the court, and the opened books. There is no hell, no underworld, no place of burning below. The heavenly throne itself is fiery and the beast slain is given over to be burned with fire.

Because the symbols in these verses are so basic and memorable, a sermon entitled "The Ancient of Days" might well be preached on the five above-mentioned attributes of God. Under judgment it might be noted that the heavenly scene which appears before Daniel in his vision is not unambiguously a final judgment at the end of history, for some beasts remain alive even though their rule is taken away (v. 12). As intimated already in chapters 2, 4 and 5, so here, the longevity of earthly rule resides ultimately with the Most High.

## One Coming, Like a Son of Man (7:13-18)

These verses are of significance for the baptism of Jesus (Matt 3:13-17; Mark 1:9-11; Luke 3:21-22; John 1:31-34), as one of the sources of two important messianic titles of Jesus ("Coming One": Matt 11:3; "Son of Man": Matt 8:20; Mark 8:31; Luke 9:58), as a source for relating Jesus' coming with the "kingdom" (Mark 1:15; cf. Matt 13:41), as a source for the belief that at the Second Coming, Jesus will come "in the clouds" (Matt 24:30; Mark 13; 16; Luke 21:17; Rev 14:14), and, as one of the sources for the belief that all nations and tongues will bow down and serve the one designated Son of Man (Phil 2:9-11; Rev 5:9-10; 7:9-12). The human author of Daniel could hardly have imagined how his words about the "One Like a Son of Man" would reverberate down through the ages: "And to him was given . . . glory and kingdom, that all peoples, nations and languages should serve him" (7:14a).

It seems likely that the original author viewed the archangel Michael as the "One like a Son of Man" and the kingdom given to him (v. 14) as a heavenly counterpart of the giving of the kingdom on earth to Israel, the saints of the Most High (v. 16). From near the beginning of the New Testament era Christians had expanded the already deep universalizing tendency of the book of Daniel by understanding the One Like a Son of Man to be Jesus, and "Israel" to be the fellowship of believers, the church (Gal 6:16). In the interpretation of Dan 7:13-18 the preacher is thus confronted with a classic example of how modern interpretation once again is apparently subversive of the preaching enterprise and of the apologetic task of the church. The olden days of preaching *were* simpler, but less challenging. Formerly (and for much conservative preaching still) what mattered most about this passage was the future and Christian application. Today there is a gain and not a loss in seeking to recapture for preaching not only Christian reinterpretation but also the original impact and meaning of the Word. This gain will not be accomplished unless the contemporary preacher acknowledges that New Testament Christian appropriation of Old

Testament passages are not always accurate indicators of the original impact of that same Old Testament passage. Accordingly a sermon "One Coming, Like a Son of Man" might be developed along the following lines.

(A) *Introduction.* (1) In his book *Truth and Method*, Hans Georg Gadamer compares the modern interpreter of the Bible to a judge who must creatively apply past legal decisions to the case before him/her. A thorough knowledge of the history of law is useful, and a clear knowledge of past precedents and landmark cases is essential. Nonetheless, the judge must creatively apply the law to the case at hand, taking all the complexities of the case into account. By no means can the judge simply repeat the words of past cases. (2) As the judge uses the history of previous legal decisions to govern his application to the case at hand, so may the interpreter in the Christian community utilize the Old and New Testaments in making applications on the requirements for action and interpretation in the present. (3) Just as the judge is grounded in past precedents and landmark decisions, and yet not hidebound by them, so must the contemporary Christian interpreter be thoroughly grounded in the Old and New Testaments and yet not permitted simply to repeat old precedents, old interpretations or the biblical texts *verbatim* as if that would constitute responsible application. (4) A reflective, thoughtful, deliberate and creative application to the situation at hand alone will constitute responsible interpretation.

(B) The *Old Testament Message*: Dominion and Kingdom will soon be given to One like a Son of Man. (1) Scholars are divided on the interpretation of this text. (2) A view favored in the light of vv. 18 and 27 (reading "people of the saints of the Most High" as a hendiadys) is that the One like a Son of Man is the historic Israel. (3) A view gaining more and more favor in the light of vv. 9, 10 and 13 (throne of God, heavenly hosts, clouds of heaven) is that the One like a Son of Man must be an angelic figure representative of Israel and therefore Michael who is elsewhere in Daniel (10:13, 21) Israel's prime, heavenly representative. (4) Regardless of whether one accepts the interpretations in items 2 or 3 above, the rule of the One like a Son of Man stands in contrast to the bestial character of the preceding reigns. (For the contemporary significance of this, see below, section D, item 6.) (5) That dominion, glory, and kingdom (v. 14) are given to the One like a Son of Man means that on earth below power, rule, and honor will be received by Israel from all nations (v. 27). (6) Historically, the respect and reception that Israel's faith and testimony to God have received among the nations have constituted at least a partial fulfillment of this prophecy. (a) Israel's faith in the universal God of justice continues to make an impact far beyond the numbers of the sons and daughters of Israel. (b) Through Judaism, Christianity, and Islam, Israel's testimony to the Creator God of justice, compassion, and providential rule continues to enjoy a worldwide acceptance.

(C) The *New Testament Message*: Jesus who is, and came, as Son of Man will come again. (1) Some New Testament scholars hold that when Jesus uses "Son of Man" with reference to himself, he is simply employing a circumlocution for "I" (so Rudolf Bultmann). (2) Others hold that the term "Son of Man" or, more properly the Aramaic *bar nasha*, was a Messianic title deliberately used by Jesus of himself to show he was not the kind of Messiah which was popularly expected (so Marie Joseph Lagrange). (3) Others see in the term "Son of Man" a title which refers to Jesus as eschatological agent ordained by God to inaugurate a new age in the present, and to bring it to consummation in the future (so Howard Kee). (4) Scholars are divided as to whether the association between suffering and the Son of Man (Mark 8:34–9:1) goes back to Jesus himself (so Vincent Taylor) or to the community which produced the Gospel (so Morton Enslin). (5) There is agreement among scholars that the title in 1 Enoch 37–82 (the so-called "Similitudes of Enoch") is used of a divine and divinely favored eschatological figure who will assume the role of judge over all the earth. In the light of 1 Enoch and Dan 7, it is plausible therefore that the title "Son of Man" in the gospels carries with it a significant overtone of one who brings divine judgment (see Matt 25:31–46). (6) No matter which of the above views one accepts or rejects, it is apparent that the title is far richer in content than a simple foil or contrast to the title Son of God. (7) With the coming of Jesus the ultimate goal of divine rule which was inaugurated at creation has entered a new and distinctive phase.

(D) The *Present Day Application*: Christian ethics can now be viewed as an interim ethics. (1) The role of the One Like a Son of Man as judge is clearly implied in the Old Testament passage and explicit in the New Testament: human beings are and will be judged by the divine for their acts. In the long haul, in the biblical view, there is no such thing as "getting away with it." (2) As Jesus, the Son of Man, suffered, so may the community of the faithful to Him expect, in this life, suffering and rebuke (Matt 5:10–12; Mark 8:34–9:1; 2 Cor 1:3–7; Col 1:24–27). (3) The extent to which any proclamation of the Gospel includes in it a sensitivity to the suffering of others may be taken as one test of the faithfulness of the preaching. (Some evangelists so stress "success" as the promised reward of faith that they leave out this important dimension. There is a danger in all Christian preaching of by-passing the Cross in favor of a direct route to the Resurrection.) (4) The present age is an interim age, between Jesus' triumphant victory over the forces of sin and death in the crucifixion and resurrection, and his coming again. This means (as Oscar Cullmann eloquently teaches in his *Christ and Time*) that we live now in the light of the decisive victory of God over the forces of evil and darkness but before the final consummation. (As the allied victories over the axis powers at El Alamein and Stalingrad were decisive victories before the final victory of World War II, so were the crucifixion and resurrection decisive victories by God over the forces of evil before the ultimate victory of the endtime, at the return of Christ.) (5) The generation that holds still to the return of Jesus as judge must be wary of giving up on the present, for we do not know the hour of coming (Matt 24:36–44). (Clarence McCartney, the great evangelical preacher of the 1920's used to say: "Christians should *plan* as if they would live forever, but *live* as if they were going to die tomorrow.") (6) Because the earthly reigns which precede that of the Son of Man, and fall under the divine judgment, are bestial in character, it falls upon the synagogue and church to labor mightily to combat the bestial character of earthly realms in favor of the humanizing tendency of the kingdom of the Son of Man. (Paul Lehman in his *Ethics in a Christian Context* convincingly sets it forth as a divine goal to labor to make life more fully human.) (7) It is part and parcel of the biblical ethic to think not only of ourselves and our own generation, but to be guided by the wisdom of past generations and to think and plan in terms of the generations yet unborn. (God's rule endures from age to age, from generation to generation. Accordingly, it is laid upon the faithful to inject the "generational dimension" into the deliberations of the body politic. In matters of domestic and foreign policy the synagogue and church have a solemn responsibility to think not only of immediate, but of the long range, results of present acts and policies. "His dominion is everlasting": Dan 7:14; see also Pss 102:18–28; 72:1–4; 90:1–2.)

## The Meek Shall Inherit the Earth/The Truth About the Fourth Beast (7:19–28)

Modern scholarship has convincingly shown that the "little horn" (v. 8), the "horn" (vv. 8, 20), and "the other (horn)" (vv. 20, 24) must be Antiochus IV Epiphanes and the specific period that of his interference with temple worship (169–167 BC). Three times in the chapter it is said that the horn has put down or uprooted three kings (vv. 8, 20, 24). It is historically accurate, as the Neo-Platonist Porphyry pointed out, that Antiochus Epiphanes defeated in battle three kings between 169 and 166 BC: King Artaxias of Armenia, Ptolemy VI Philometor, and Ptolemy VII Euergetes. Even this obviously correct identification is not without its problems, for the context of vv. 8 and 20 suggest that the three horns (vv. 8, 20) or "kings" (v. 24) may have been intended by the original author to have belonged to the ten horns which preceded. Then the match would not be perfect. Louis Hartman, in the Anchor Bible, solves the problem by positing that the ten horns were not predecessors but contemporaries or "fellows" of the little horn as v. 20 explicitly states. Daniel wishes "to know the truth" (Aramaic "to make certain") concerning the fourth beast. This desire could be explored in a sermon, "The Truth about the Fourth Beast." The outline of such a sermon might proceed as follows.

(A) Identification of the *Dramatis Personnae*. (1) The Ancient of Days (v. 23) is God (as in v. 13). (The title itself is old, going back at least to the "Father of Years" figure who appears in the fourteenth-century Ugaritic texts.) (2) The "court" sitting in judgment (v. 26) is the heavenly court (as in v. 10). (3) Contemporary scholarship has made the identification of the horn of vv. 20, 24 virtually certain. (Antiochus IV Epiphanes was the Hellenistic leader who made war on Judaea, persecuted the saints and effected a cessation of the regular sacrifices as we know from 1 Maccabees 1.) (4) The "saints" against whom the horn makes war (v. 21) are most probably the pious ones in Judaea (although some scholars hold they are angelic representatives of the nation Israel rather than the nation itself). (5) The ten kings (ten horns) of v. 24 and three kings (horns) of vv. 8, 20, 24 are ten contemporaries of Antiochus IV.

(B) The major offenses of the beast were religious: (1) He persecuted the saints: v. 25a. (The awful policies and practices of Antiochus not only included cessation of the regular offerings and holocaust-sacrifices but a deliberate attempt to force a Hellenistic way of life and worship on the Jewish community [1 Maccabees 1–5; 2 Maccabees 4–6].) (2) He intended to change the feast days (lit. times) and the law: v. 25b. (The very wording of this verse and use of the so-called prophetic perfect shows the author's confidence that the repressive policies of Antiochus would not ultimately be successful. Not only did the latter prohibit celebration of the sabbath and the keeping of the traditional feasts [2 Maccabees 6:6], he evidently also condoned an imposition of a different calendar by which the feast days would be reckoned. The instruments of this intended "alteration" were obviously the Hellenizing high priests whom he installed: Jason and Menelaus; see 2 Maccabees 4–6.) (3) The biblical writer was confident that the duration of the persecution would be no longer than three and a half years: v. 25c. (Part of the assurance he receives from the angelic intermediary, v. 23, foretells a definite terminus to the present tribulation. See also the calculations in 8:13–19 and the sermon suggested there.)

(C) Those living in North America are not threatened by such threats of religious persecution: the threatening beast is of a different sort. (1) Persecution and repression on religious grounds is wide-spread today and not only in the Soviet Union. (2) The hard won heritage of freedom of religious expression is one for which we may be immensely grateful. (3) The beast that threatens us in North America is not overtly oppressive but subtler and more insidious: the pursuit of pleasure and self-gratification untempered by even our own religious restraints. (4) Much confession of sin today has become routinized and vague. (5) We have forgotten the lessons of our own theologians that the human spirit is capable of infinite self-deception. (See especially the works of Reinhold Niebuhr and Langdon Gilkey.) (6) Even the institution of the church has become largely an instrument for individual solace, a haven for therapy. (7) Rather than speaking to our hearts and consciences, much contemporary preaching is self-congratulatory to congregations for their bounty. (8) The way back to a deeper, less callous and less narcissistic faith is to be found through examining: (i) *God's* bounty to us; (ii) the social and psychological depths of human greed, *inordinate* self-love, and self-deception; and (iii) the social, communal and political ways in which the divine commandment of love may be put into practice. ("He who says he is in the light and has no compassion for (lit. hates) his brother is in the darkness still": 1 John 2:9.)

A sermon based on Dan 7:27 entitled "The Meek Shall Inherit the Earth" might go as follows.

(A) Daniel's vision of the Kingdom and its greatness being given to the saints has its parallels elsewhere in the Old Testament and the New. (1) The vision in Dan 7 is of a cessation of persecution with the heavenly courts deciding in favor of an earthly rule for Israel. (The vision arose in a time of severe harassment, interference with the cultus, and pressures to paganize on pain of death.) (2) Zephaniah more than four centuries before the Antiochene persecutions similarly prophesied that the haughty would be removed but the humble and lowly remain (Zeph 3:11–12). (3) And nearly a century before that, Isaiah of Jerusalem similarly prophesied a humbling of the haughty and a grazing of the lambs among the ruins (Isa 5:13–17). (4) Jesus in the Sermon on the Mount, some 200 years after Daniel, reiterates the same prophetic theme: "Blessed are the meek for they shall inherit the earth" (Matt 5:5).

(B) The prophecy of Isaiah, Zephaniah, Daniel and Jesus seems to be utter folly for everyone knows that money counts and power prevails. (1) In many instances it is true that temporal power prevails. (Missionaries to El Salvador relate how in 1978–79 after peasant leaders had volunteered to serve as managers in proposed measures for land re-distribution, those same volunteers were methodically assassinated within three weeks of the speaking out.) (2) Since Charles Darwin it is axiomatic that the fittest survive and not the meek. (Events and theory would thus seem to contradict the validity of the biblical maxim.) (3) Nonetheless, evil, unmitigated greed, and an unrestrained exercise of political power seem also inexorably to lead to self-destruction, rebellion of the suppressed, and to an ultimate demise. (Hitler did not ultimately prevail; the racial subjugation of the blacks in South Africa will not endure as it did not in the United States; the reign of terror of Idi Amin did not abide; and, similarly, a mindless or incautious development of nuclear power is bound to boomerang and make inheritance of the earth difficult if not literally impossible for our offspring.) (4) Only those who are humble enough to live with some restraint, criticism of self, and sensitivity to others will endure. (5) This foolish maxim belongs to the wisdom of God. (6) Sadly, an American foreign policy untempered by humility in its mounting of military power will as inexorably demonstrate the hard truth of another biblical maxim: everyone who lives by the sword will die by the sword (Matt 26:52). (Reliance upon military power to the virtual exclusion of a consideration of morality, justice and other avenues of political suasion demonstrates at once a crude arrogance, a lack of imagination, an ability to see only human bestiality rather than nobility, and a palpable lack of faith in the God whose will it is to establish justice and righteousness; see also Isa 31:1; 30:15.)

# Apocalyptic Made Plain
## (Daniel 8:1–27)

Dan 8 would be a good chapter with which to commence a series of sermons on Daniel. It contains a number of the standard elements of apocalyptic: An enigmatic vision, animal symbolism, history told in veiled terms, angels, persecution, prediction, and interpretation of the vision. Further, in this chapter the angel Gabriel reveals to Daniel that historic figures symbolized by the two-horned ram and the he-goat respectively are Persia-Media and Greece (vv. 20–21). A solid foundation for interpreting apocalyptic can thus be laid in preaching from this chapter.

The chapter quite naturally subdivides into three parts: vision (vv. 1–12), introduction of heavenly interpreters (vv. 13–19), interpretation of the vision (vv. 20–27).

## The Interpretation of Apocalyptic (8:1–8)

These verses should be read together with vv. 15–21 which introduce the heavenly interpreters (vv. 15–19) and their interpretation (vv. 20–21). Susa was the chief capital not of the Babylonian, but of the Persian Empire. It was destroyed in 645 BC and was not rebuilt until 521 BC at the beginning of the reign of Darius I (522–486 BC). The reference to Susa thus hardly suits the conservative and orthodox interpretation that the Daniel of this chapter, in any event, has a very solid grounding in history. On the other hand, both Babylon and Susa were under the control of the Greco-Syrians (Seleucids) at the time of the Maccabean Revolt. Indeed, Antiochus the Great, the grandfather of Antiochus IV was killed in Susa in 187 BC while in the process of plundering the temple of Bel. A sermon on "The Interpretation of Apocalyptic" might be developed along the following lines.

(A) Symbolic visions are a regular feature of apocalyptic. (1) The vision of the ram and he-goat are symbols taken from the Zodiac (Aries and Capricorn). (a) Aries is the zodiacal sign of the Spring Equinox (March 21–April 20) and because two-horned, an appropriate symbol of the two-sectioned

Kingdom of the Medes and Persians. Herodotus relates some fascinating though blood curdling tales of Cyrus' acquisition of the kingdom of the Medes (*Histories*, Book I, 113–130). (b) Capricorn is the zodiacal sign of the Winter Equinox (December 22–January 20) and here a symbol of Greece. (2) Apocalyptic tells history through the use of symbols. (a) In this chapter the following three events are told symbolically: (i) Alexander the Great's victory over the Medes and Persians (the he-goat with one great horn vs. the two-horned ram); (ii) the death of Alexander and his replacement by four of his generals (four horns replace the one); (iii) the religious persecution of the Jewish community by Antiochus IV Epiphanes (the little horn which magnified itself: vv. 9–11). (b) In chapter 11 a more detailed survey is symbolically given from Alexander the Great on down to Antiochus IV. (3) This method of telling history has its roots in the Old Testament (see Gen 49, e.g., where different animals symbolize the tribes and Ezek 15 where the Babylonian Exile is symbolized by an eagle's snipping off the top of a cedar tree and carrying it to a distant land). (4) There can be no mistaking the correctness of the identification of the symbols in vv. 1–8: they are identified in vv. 20–21. (5) The symbols in chapters 2, 4 and 11 similarly can be identified with past, historic kings and kingdoms. (6) The attractive tendency to update these symbolic figures is mistaken. (It is a process born of the desire to find in the Bible a crystal ball which will unfold wondrous clues of events soon to transpire.)

(B) Because we can learn from history, we can learn from apocalyptic. (1) The education of Alexander the Great under the tutelage of the great philosopher, Aristotle, his family background, and talents all contain clues to his remarkable success. (2) The (relatively early) death of Alexander and succession by four of his generals remind us of the waxing and waning, the rise and fall of empires and of great leaders. (3) The demise of the arrogant Antiochus IV, predicted in this chapter (v. 25) may serve as a reminder to those under persecution that the duration of the tyrant is not forever.

(C) To ignore the historical interpretation of apocalyptic (and thus to sweep aside the intelligent interpretation of the Scripture) would be to fall prey to the temptation to govern our lives by magic rather than by the use of reason and a searching faith. (1) It would be comforting to think that the Bible could be read as a secret code into the events of our own time (but it would be mistaken). (2) The results of the historical interpretation of the Scripture have been achieved at the cost of great effort and painstaking research. (The results are not perfect, but approximate, in need of constant modification.) (3) To take seriously the "Crystal Ball" view of the apocalyptic writings such as Daniel would be tantamount to advising a planning of one's life on the basis of the daily horoscope in the newspapers. (4) Settling for anything less than a reasonable faith would constitute a retreat into primitivism and magic. (a) The Hebrew word for repentance (*teshubah* = lit. "turning") suggests that faith seeking guidance will reexamine its mental outlook. (b) Faith in God does not mean a sacrifice of the intellect but a quickening of its exercise through turning to God. (5) A faith which turns to God will seek to learn from the past, from secular history, and especially from the Bible.

## Deprivation and Discovery (8:9–12)

For the sake of continuity, these verses should be read together with vv. 13–17 and 22–27.

It is often so that only when someone or something has been taken away do we realize how much that missing one or thing has meant to us. So it was for the author of Daniel. When the regular temple offerings (the *tamidim*: v. 11) were interrupted, it was to him as if "truth was cast down to the ground" (v. 12). The interrupter was Antiochus IV Epiphanes. He invaded Jerusalem, plundered the sanctuary and brought a halt to sacrificial worship (see 1 Maccabees). Accordingly, a sermon might be developed along the following lines.

(A) Deprivation may lead to discovery. (1) A young man or woman may discover in a hurry how much a person of the opposite sex means to him/her when a once close relationship is threatened or dissolved. (2) The death of a friend or loved one, divorce, or the moving away of someone with whom one has been close, may also have the same effect. (3) Fasting or abstaining from solid foods enables one soon to discern how the hungry lack reserves of energy for vigorous physical effort. (4) In Daniel's time the author witnessed the desecration of the sanctuary and proscription of presentation of the regular burnt offerings. (This deprivation led to a deeper awareness that the regular sacrificial worship mattered to him very much.)

(B) Sacrifices—the physical slaughtering of animals—is a practice no longer observed in Judaism or in Christian churches, yet without being deprived of our worship, there is much we can learn about it by looking at the Old Testament view of sacrifices. (1) There are three main ways in which sacrifices are conceived in the Old Testament: (a) *As gifts*. (i) The tithe and the whole burnt offerings *(oloth)* were understood in this fashion, as gifts or tribute given to the divine. (ii) In the same way that the one who gave gifts to a human overlord would expect protection in return for his demonstration of allegiance, so the worshiper in Israel received assurance from giving that the Overlord of All would watch over and take special care of him. (iii) Gratitude and joy as well as expectation were important motifs—joyously returning to God a token of thanksgiving (a wave offering, a first fruit, or a basket of produce) in response to His bounty (see Deut 16:9–15; 26:1–4). (b) *As a means of communion*. (i) In some of the offerings such as the so-called "peace offerings" (= "shared offerings": *NEB*) or "offerings of well-being": *NJV)* the worshiper would partake of what has been offered to God (at the altar) and also share with the poor and Levites. (ii) He/she was thus given a sense of communion, of sharing with the divine inasmuch as the portion of the offering on the altar symbolized the part set aside for God. (iii) When offerings were accompanied by a vow, the worshiper's partaking was in effect a sacramental meal understood to be an affirmation of loyalty and a sign and seal of fellowship. (c) *As a means of atonement or expiation*. (i) The "guilt offering" (= "reparation offering": *IDB Supplementary Volume*) and "sin offering" (= "purgation offering": *IDB Supplementary Volume)* were offerings of this type. The former was given as something of a fine or reparation to compensate for an offense. The latter was given to cover or to purge away (Heb. *kapar*) sins committed unknowingly. (ii) In the slaying of the passover lamb the idea is present that the blood shed, if sprinkled or smeared on the doorposts, would cause the Destroyer to turn away and pass over the house so marked. (iii) The one appeased was not the Destroyer or some evil spirit but the Lord Himself who controlled the Destroyer (Exod 12:23). (iv) Behind these sacrifices and also behind the offering of the scapegoat (Lev 16), is the idea that Yahweh's wrath is aroused by sin and that some form of reparation or atonement had to be made. (v) Psychologically there was tremendous profundity to this whole sacrificial system because it provided a way of dramatizing the immensely destructive power of guilt if unatoned. These sacrifices thus expressed at once the seriousness of human wrong doing in the eyes of God and also that God had graciously provided a way for restitution and recovery of wholeness. (vi) Sensible modern churchmen and women do not call for a reinstitution of the sacrificial system but they will see that the ancient Israelite insights into the human psyche remain valid: if human beings sin, some outward, symbolic act of reparation may be a useful instrument for the restoration of mental and emotional health.

(C) The Cross—the place of the sacrificial death of Jesus—may similarly serve as a reminder of how even petty sins may be death-bringing and that what God requires of us now are the sacrifices of a broken and contrite heart. (1) Well-meaning people through gossip, innuendo, and bigotry can be directly instrumental in destroying others. (This is vividly illustrated in the classic novel by Patrick White, *Riders in the Chariot*.) (2) The Cross reminds us that even well-meaning religious leaders today can all too easily fall into supporting the persecution and purgation from society (i.e., death?) of certain "undesirable elements." (The Bible, on the contrary, teaches continually the divine love of the sinner but hatred of the sin.) (3) Now that the sacrificial system is over and that the death of Jesus is many years behind us, what God requires still is a spirit of contriteness (awareness of fallibility) and humility (a conquering of the spirit of self-congratulation.) (See Ps 51:15-19.) (4) When such sacrifices are offered the modern man and woman will also become aware of a new wholeness and power dependent not on status, wealth, or worldly success but upon the spirit of the Creator and Redeemer of all.

## Predictions and Hope (8:13–19)

In verses 13-19 we encounter the second main division of the chapter, introduction of the heavenly interpreters. For the first time in the book an angel is mentioned by name (v. 16). Gabriel means "Hero of God." The response of Daniel to the theophany, or more correctly, angelophany is similar to that of Isaiah of Jerusalem before the divine holiness, namely, one of reverence and contrite worship. For a sermon on angels, see above under 4:19-27, "Outlaw Angels?"

In verses 13-14 Daniel overhears a heavenly dialogue in which one angel says to another "For how long will this transgression that makes desolate last?" The answer he receives is: it will be 2300 evenings and mornings before the sanctuary is restored. The prediction is precise—as are the predictions in 9:25-27; 12:6-7; and 12:11-12. The three afore-mentioned passages and verses 13-14 furnish a good case in point to demonstrate that even the angels soon find it necessary to modify predictive timetables concerning the endtime of human woes. Many similar examples from modern history could be given. The presence in Scripture of predictions such as these raise the question: how central are the predictions of the Bible to the biblical message? A sermon on "Prediction and Hope" might be developed along the following lines.

(A) The Bible unquestionably contains many predictions. How should we view them? How central are they to the faith? (1) Some predictions are of a general nature, such as Ezek 34, that the sheep of Israel will be scattered but God will gather them together again, sending a shepherd after His own heart. (2) Some are promissory, containing the promise of divine action in the near future or distant future—such as Ezek 37 and the promise to raise up Israel from the dust through the activity of His reviving spirit, or Jer 31 with its promise to write the law upon human hearts. (3) Some predictions are extremely specific, such as those in Dan 7:25-27; 8:13-14; 12:6-7, 11-12. (4) Some passages such as Isa 53 and Dan 11 have been interpreted as predictions of the future by some but as descriptions of past events by others. (Each such disputed passage must be examined carefully in form and context before the individual comes to his or her own conclusion.) (5) Many passages in the Old Testament were understood by New Testament writers to be examples of predictions fulfilled in the life of Jesus of Nazareth. (6) The modern Christian may affirm the Messiahship and Lordship

of Jesus without insisting that every one of the passages understood to be original predictions by the New Testament
writers must have been such. (The modern Christian interpreter will thus allow that originally descriptive passages
such as Isa 53 or Dan 9:25–27 have been given a predictive
interpretation which they may not have originally had.) (a)
This does *not* mean that the modern Christian denies every
prediction of Christ in the Old Testament. (b) This *does* mean
that some of the passages predictively interpreted may not
*originally* have been intended as such by the original writers.
(7) In sum, predictions are present in the Bible (both Testaments) which vary in specificity and certainty. (8) We would
miss the point of the Old Testament, however, if we viewed it
primarily as a Book of Predictions rather than as a Guide-
book to Fullness of Life and a Pointer to Hope.

(B) Some predictions such as those in Dan 8:13–14;
12:6–7, 11–12 are born in times of stress and persecution. (1)
The abolition of temple offerings was perceived to be a grave
disaster. The author wished earnestly for this situation to be
corrected. (2) Prediction of the duration of the period of deso-
lation is pronounced four times by a heavenly agent: 1150
days (8:13); an additional 128 days = $3^1/2$ years (12:6–7); an
additional 12 days beyond that = 1290 days (12:11); and an
additional 45 days beyond that = 1335 days (12:12). (3) The
fact that adjustment had to be made is a strong indication of
the authenticity and genuineness of the figures. (4) One is reminded of the successive predictions made with respect to
the release date of the American hostages in Iran. (5) The
temptation is ever present to want to be able to predict the
answers to such questions as "How long will the martial law
last in country X?" "When will the civil and military conflict
in country Y come to an end?" (6) As a rule the Bible does not
supply answers as specific as those supplied in these
passages. (7) Rather it looks to the future in hope. (8) It is to
the more usual biblical response we should look in times of
stress rather than to passages like 8:14.

(C) The function performed by the specific predictions in
8:14 is to bring hope to the author and his Audience. (1) Of
the three most celebrated theological virtues, hope (though
perhaps least stressed) is the most vital ("Faith is the foundation upon which hope rests, hope nourishes and sustains

faith": John Calvin.) (2) In times of stress and privation hope enables the human being to endure without being crushed. ("Hope makes us ready to bear 'the cross of the present' ": Jürgen Moltmann.) (3) In times of apparent flourishing, hope provides an antidote against stagnation and holds out the promise of renewal. ("Creative action springing from faith is impossible without new thinking and planning that springs from hope": Moltmann.) (4) Hope serves as a powerful stimulus to the believer to strive to bring into reality the implementation of the law of love. ("The theologian is concerned not merely to supply a different *interpretation* of the world, of history and of human nature, but to *transform* them in expectation of a divine transformation": Moltmann.) (5) Even though the predictions in Daniel are modified—evidently as delays came in the defeat of Antiochus IV Epiphanes—the predictions constitute injections of hope into the bleak world of a community deprived of its accustomed formal worship. (6) So worship today should kindle within us hope in the divine power to transform corrupt social institutions and perverse human hearts.

## Solutions to Historic Dilemmas (8:20–27)

Interpretations of the enigmatic visions of 8:1-12 are given in vv. 20–27. As we saw earlier in the discussion of 2:1-11, the Aramaic word *peshar* very likely meant not only "to interpret" but also "to solve," and "to remove the evil consequence of." So here the interpretation not only identifies the symbols of vv. 1-11 but also removes the threat and the force of the one symbolized by the "little horn" by pronouncing that it had done its worse and soon would be broken itself by no human hand. The interpretation furnished is thus at the same time a solution. A sermon on these verses might explore the subject of "Solutions."

(A) Not all of life's dilemmas will be as baffling as the historic symbolism of 8:1-11. (1) Unlike Mr. K. in Kafka's *The Trial*, we may be able to identify with greater precision the nature of the ills that assail us. (2) In the same way that this chapter unfolds, there is a historic-social dimension to many of the problems that confront us. (3) Part of the fault the interpretation finds with the king who arises in the latter days is his destructiveness and that he rises up even against The Prince of Princes. (The Scripture thus suggests that arrogance, wanton destructiveness, and sacrilege will not endure.)

(B) In this chapter an interpretation to enigmatic symbolism is given. (1) Even though the dream-like quality of apocalyptic may not be part of the dilemmas that confront us, there are several aspects underlying the symbolism which remain pertinent. (2) Sound analysis of any of our dilemmas will soon take us back to consideration of their historic-social roots. (3) Persons of forthrightness and discernment may knowingly or unknowingly inflict harm on others. (4) Persons may prosper through the use of deceit, and self-congratulations may be multiplied but such will not endure.

(C) There is a sovereign who rules over all history. (1) Just as the tyrant may strike down others without warning, so may the divine sovereign with seemingly little or no human preparation bring about the demise of a tyrant. (2) Historic and social analyses are indispensable in coming to solutions of problems that beset us. (3) Politically we must strive to avoid systems that foster arrogance and allow the exercise of destructive use of power with impunity. (4) It is plain that the author of Daniel did not favor regicide, for the course of history he held to be in the Almighty's hands. (Regicides are described in the Bible: 2 Kings 8:7–15; 9:21–26, 30–37; 10:1–11; 11:1–20; but they are as a rule condemned rather than enjoined; see Hosea 1:4–5.) (5) Though all of the vision and its interpretation may not have been entirely clear, Daniel carried on with the human king's business. (6) The author claims that Daniel did not understand the vision and was appalled by it (v. 27). It is apparent, however, that he understood more than he let on. (The interpretation furnished a solution which at once enabled Daniel to cope and to hope.)

# Prophetic Prediction and Prayer
## (Daniel 9:1–27)

Dan 9 easily divides into two parts: vv. 1–2, 20–27 center on the prophecy of Jer 25:11–14 and 29:10 that the exile would last seventy years, and vv. 3–19 contain a beautiful prayer of confession, lamentation and supplication.

## Darius and Midrash (9:1–2, 20–27)

Verse 1 contains a genuine historical reflection which is generally, but not precisely, accurate. Darius I (522–486 BC) the son of Hystaspes was the father of Ahasuerus (Xerxes). Darius is known and celebrated as the Persian king who first invaded Greece and was repulsed by the greatly outnumbered Greeks at the Battle of Marathon in 490 BC. He was a great lawgiver who had the reputation of stern justice and little toleration for corruption among his judges. He captured Babylon, the capital city of the Chaldeans, fairly early on in his reign, and made his administrative capital in Susa in the region of Media. Darius recorded his exploits in stone, in the famous Behistun Inscription which he had carved 500 feet above the Kirmanshah Plain, 65 miles east of Babylon in the Iranian plateau. The inscription was written in Persian, Elamite and Akkadian, and in the mid 1800's AD proved to be the key for unlocking Akkadian, the language of the Assyrians and the Babylonians.

In vv. 1–2 and 20–27 the author's fascination with the predictive side of prophecy reaches its height. Not only did he feel that in a general way the prophecies of Isaiah of Babylon were being fulfilled in his day among young Judeans serving in foreign courts, such as we saw was the case in chapters 2–6, he now turns to Jer 25:11–14 and 29:10 as furnishing a reliable timetable for the events of his own day. What was an implicit midrash (expansion of a scriptural text) in chapters 1–6 becomes here an explicit midrash. Once again the reasoning of our author seems to be nearly, but not altogether, on the mark. It is difficult for us to put ourselves into the shoes of the ancient author and to be certain it is his shoes we are putting on. There is wide agreement in any event on the following points. (1) The prophecy of Jeremiah about the 70-year exile for some reason attracted his attention as it did the Chronicler's (2 Chron 36:15–21). It seems likely that the original reason rested in the fact that taken as a literal prophecy it was remarkably well fulfilled. (The city of Jerusalem fell to the Babylonians in 587/86 BC and approximately 70 years later the temple which had been destroyed was rebuilt.) (2) The author of Dan 1 and 9, however, considered that the exile began in the third year of the reign of Nebuchadnezzar, i.e., in 606 BC (see Daniel 1:1). This means that, unless otherwise stipulated, the base point of reckoning must be not 587/86 but 606 BC (3) The author reinterprets the originally successful prophecy of Jeremiah to apply to his day by suggesting that the 70 years meant 70 weeks of years, i.e., 490 years (9:20). (4) In the year 172 BC Onias III, the son of the great high priest Simon, was assassinated. It appears quite certain that Onias III was the "anointed one" who was "cut off" according to 9:26. (The arithmetic bears out this identification: 62 weeks [of years] equals 434 years; 606 less 434 equals 172 [BC].) (5) The prediction "The people of the prince who is to come shall destroy the city and the sanctuary" (9:26) would then be a reference to the attack upon the city and the desecrations of the sanctuary committed by Antiochus IV Epiphanes. (6) The prediction that the offering would be cut off for one half week (9:27) would thus mean a predicted three and a half years. Since we know from 1 Maccabees 1:20–63 that the desolations began in 169 BC and that the offerings were cut off in 167 BC, it seems safe to conclude that the last stage of the book was written some time after 167 BC and before the rededication of the temple.

Other points in the author's arithmetic do not appear as plain to us and do not seem to fit so neatly. The preacher may be well advised not to dwell overly much in sermon on the specifics of the prediction. The sermon suggested above in chapter 8 on "Predictions and Hope" could easily be adapted to suit the predictions of chapter nine.

## Preparation for Prayer (9:3–6)

These four verses could constitute the basis for the introductory sermon in a series of four based on the prayer of 9:4–19. The entire prayer follows the pattern of the lamentations in the Psalms which are far and away the most numerous single type in the Psalter. Lacking only in this lamentation is the "assurance of hearing," namely, the worshiper's utterance of the certainty that he has been heard. The deep faith of the prayer is so evident that it may be argued that this element is implied in the unmistakable affirmations of God's tender mercies and forgiveness (v. 9).

The style of the prayer is "synagogal." Note especially the many majestic synonyms of God. As Lacocque points out, the prayer "became a part of the official Jewish liturgy for the daily morning office and for days of fasting, particularly Yom Kippur." Because there are no Aramaisms in it and because it draws especially heavily on Jeremiah and Deuteronomy, a strong case has been made that the prayer is a liturgical fragment from the 600's BC. For a comparable prayer see Neh 9.

Many classics on prayer will furnish for sermons ample illustrative and quotable material. For those which have been especially helpful to me, see my comments on 6:10–18. A sermon which focusses on vv. 3–6, "Preparation For Prayer," might take the following shape.

(A) There are prayers of many kinds for most of which, except the most spontaneous, some form of spiritual and even physical preparation is needed. (1) The types of prayer are several: adoration and praise, ascription of greatness, confession, thanksgiving, intercession and supplication, and petition. (2) What is the purpose of prayer? (a) Certainly not simply to go through motions, to satisfy social convention. (b) But rather, become more closely attuned to the divine love and power, (c) to avail ourselves of a tremendous avenue to strength, and (d) to make ourselves more open to the urgings of the divine to ministry and service. (3) No matter what the type or purpose, some preparation is usually needed. (a) *Daniel turned his face to God:* that means some form of turning away from direct address with other human beings, some form of getting to a place apart. (b) *Daniel fasted:* recent experience of going on a liquid diet on Mondays has shown me how much a form of fasting will quicken the mind, make one more aware of the limits of his energies and facilitate a thinking of the hungry and destitute. (Speak from your own experience.) (c) *Daniel put on sackcloth:* the selection of clothing suitable for confession and penitence is culturally determined. It may be, however, that for us when attired in pajamas in morning and evening prayer we would be more conscious of our physical vulnerability and closeness to the nakedness of infancy and of the grave. (d) *Daniel uses ashes*: some physical sign was employed for his own and (presumably also in part) other's benefit. The posture or physical bearing and attitude of the suppliant may substitute. Before God in the privacy of one's own chambers no need to refrain from kneeling, standing, sitting, or raising up one's arms in accordance with the prayer being expressed. (4) *Summary*: Daniel's turning his face to God constituted his spiritual preparation; his fasting in sackcloth and ashes constituted his physical preparation. Daniel sought God.

(B) The recollection of the character, attributes, and past acts of God. (1) The prayer of 9:4–19 is largely confessional, but even in confession the models of prayer do not commence with "I" but with "Thou"—the Divine Thou. (2) The greatness and fearsomeness of God are mentioned first. (a) We moderns may have retained and even have enhanced our sense of the greatness of God thanks to the telescope and microscope which are only beginning to unfold to us the wonders of the heavens and of the minute forms of life. (b) We in the West have nearly lost, however, the sense of the fearsomeness of God. We have tamed nature, fought an amazingly successful battle against disease, and have learned how to insulate ourselves from the elements. Death from flood, famine, fire, war still strikes, but most of us have been spared. We so easily take life for granted, and God is less fearsome: death is once removed. (3) Daniel next remembers God's covenant and steadfast love, the divine loyalty to those who have been loyal to Him. The covenant is made on the basis of the divine grace and kept out of divine mercy and kindness with those who have loved God and have been faithful in following the divine imperatives. (4) Such recollections are a fitting way to commence prayer of any sort.

(C) Confession takes place. (1) With an enumeration of specific kinds of sins: (a) "We have sinned"—literally "missed the mark." (The underlying idea is that life is a walking, each decision a step and the individual who fails to attain the goal, destination, or target of morality and decency has "sinned."); (b) "we have done wrong"—literally "acted perversely or crookedly." (The underlying idea is similar to the above, of trespassing or going to one side or the other of a path, hence, deviation.); (c) "we have acted wickedly"—literally "committed evil." (The underlying idea is the committing of ungodly or unrighteous acts.); (d) "we have rebelled." (The underlying idea is an overthrow of authority and renunciation of the legitimacy of the exercise of claims of authority—in this instance, against God.); (e) "we have turned aside from Thy commandments and ordinances." (The underlying idea is again one of movement or walking away from the express oral and written guidance of God.); (f) "we have not listened to Thy servants the prophets who spoke in Thy name." (The underlying idea is that the people of Daniel's time had turned deaf ears on the words uttered by Yahweh's spokesmen on His authority to kings, princes, kinsmen, and nobles.) (2) The confession is corporate: "we" . . . "our." (3) So, if our prayer is to follow this pattern and be sincere, it must also be corporate—think not only of individual shortcomings but of social ills and malpractices—and be specific. At this point the preacher may wish to fill in the blanks, that is, begin to elucidate specific social offenses which his/her faith and experience suggest might properly be mentioned in a prayer of confession. (For a list of modern idols, see the sermon suggested above under 3:1-12, "The Dimensions of Idolatry.")

## At the Heart of Prayer (9:7-8)

In a recent article on prayer Father Roland E. Murphy, the distinguished Roman Catholic scholar who teaches at the Duke Divinity School, recalled having read somewhere the epigram: "Loben ist Leben" ('To praise is to live"). The idea is that praise is an important emphasis within every community which counts the Bible among its rich treasures and that the praise of God fosters and nourishes fullness of human life. The praise of God lies close to the heart of life and of prayer. Verses 7-8 furnish three clues on the dimensions of prayer. A sermon, "At the Heart of Prayer," might be developed along the following lines.

(A) Praise is central. (1) Daniel attributes righteousness to God. (2) Recent study has shown that the righteousness (*tsedakah*) of God refers primarily to His conduct and creative acts which are aimed at establishing order, salvation, wholeness, and redemption for humankind (see Ps 119:142;

Isa 51:6, 8; 59:16, 17; 60:17). (3) Ascribing righteousness to
God is thus tantamount to praising Him not only for a stance
and attitude which desires to establish order and wholeness
among humankind but also for acting to bring it to pass (see
especially Ps 96). (4) "Shame of face" is confessed because
Daniel acknowledges his and his people's failure to display
the human righteousness and pursuit of orderly conduct
which the divine righteousness wills.

(B) Next to the vertical, there is also a horizontal dimension to prayer: it moves from praise to God to concern for
one's fellow human beings—near and far. (1) In his classic
book on *Prayer*, Friedrich Heiler cites the social awareness of
the worshiper as distinctive of biblical, and especially prophetic, prayer. (2) The author of this prayer here shows an
awareness not only of his own fellow inhabitants of the city
of Jerusalem, but also of Judah and those dispersed in Exile
to distant lands. (3) He acknowledges it is because of their
treachery (RSV), lit. unfaithfulness and acting contrary to
duty, which has motivated God so to disperse them.

(C) There is an internal dimension and an inward movement in prayer. (1) "Confusion of face" means literally "a
shame of face." (2) This means an acknowledgment not so
much that one stands embarrassed before other human beings for having "missed the mark" morally but before God
and in one's own self-awareness. (3) Spiritual maturity is
thus marked by counting shortcomings before God and one's
self as of equal, if not greater, seriousness as shortcomings
which come to the attention of others. (4) Even in the inward
movement one does not cast blame on others but may simply
acknowledge a complicity, a sharing of guilt ("To us, O Lord,
belongs shame of face, to our kings, to our princes and to our
fathers"). (5) A central attitudinal feature of this prayer may
be characterized as praise of God sufficiently self-forgetful to
think of one's fellow human beings who are in a worse or
similar plight, and thus to be sufficiently humble to acknowledge one's own sin and sufficiently free to acknowledge the
extent to which other leaders have also been involved. (6)
This humility is not a false humility because the petitioner
neither exaggerates nor underplays the magnitude and depth
of his own moral shortcomings in relation to his fellow
citizens.

## Personal Prayer (9:9–14)

The intensely personal aspect of this prayer is expressed in deeply social, rather than individualistic, terms. Spiritual narcissism, becoming enamoured of the contemplation of the portrait of one's own individual spiritual pilgrimmage, is not a form of spirituality fostered by the Bible. The saints of the Bible travel in the company of other pilgrims and pray without losing that sense of identification with one's own people.

(A) Recollection of the "tender compassion" and forgiveness of God are characteristic of biblical prayer. (1) The word *rachamin*, mercy (RSV) or mercies (KJV), is taken from the Hebrew word for womb (*racham*); hence the word might be rendered "maternal compassion"; the fact that it is a plural suggests continued and repeated acts of love. (2) The petitioner thus attributes compassion, deep feeling, *pathos* to God. (3) Abraham Joshua Heschel has suggested that the prophet is one who had deep empathy with the divine compassion. (The prophet thus does not dispassionately pronounce the divine word [of judgment or hope] but very much identifies himself with the pathos which underlies the divine word.) (4) So the woman and man of prayer will be mindful of the parent–mother love of God which cannot and does not cease. (5) The word forgiveness in Hebrew is also a plural, thus literally, "forgivenesses" or "pardons." (The petitioner recalls how God repeatedly pardons offenses.)

(B) This model of biblical prayer also acknowledges the rightful authority of God. (1) The petitioner cites rebellion as his offense and that of his people. Thus he admits that the exercise of authority properly belongs to God. (2) The petitioner cites disobedience to the voice of God as his offense and that of his people. (3) The petitioner cites his and his people's failure to follow God's laws or instructions (lit. *toroth*) as his offense and his people's. (4) The petitioner acknowledges that even though the laws were delivered by the prophets, God's servants, he and the people have crossed over the limits placed on them by the law. (5) "All Israel" has thus wilfully turned aside and refused to heed the divine voice.

(C) This model of biblical prayer acknowledges that many personal calamities which have befallen the people were deserved. (1) Reference is made to the Mosaic law and the curses in it which are stipulated as ones which will come if the laws are not followed (see especially Deut 28). (2) The petitioner holds that he and his people were already forewarned of the disaster which would be brought upon the nation, rulers, and city of Jerusalem for non-compliance to the law. (3) Thus the biblical model of prayer does not place primary blame for ills upon demonic external forces, but upon a merciful yet just God who rules with an order and predictability.

## The Right Name for Prayer (9:15–19)

Verses 20–23 constitute a bridge between the prayer and the interpretation of the prophecy. These verses might well be included in any reading for they provide a fitting and touching episode of the divine response to the prayer.

The concluding verses in the prayer center around the theme of *name* (vv. 15, 18, 19). Other themes struck earlier in the prayer are here reiterated: the contrast between God's mercy and Israel's sin (v. 18), petition for forgiveness (v. 19), explicit mention of the city (vv. 16, 18, 19), and reference to specific gracious acts of God (v. 15). A sermon might be built around the new theme under the title "The Right Name for Prayer" along the following lines.

(A) In the prayer of the biblical faith, the name of God is the Alpha and Omega, the Beginning and the End. (1) At the outset of prayer, as here, the divine is addressed by name. (2) At the conclusion of prayer, as in "in the name of Jesus Christ our Lord," the name of God is also frequently cited. (3) There is a name-theology in prayer. Name may mean: (a) reputation, fame (as in v. 15, the reputation God established through effecting a deliverance at the exodus); (b) a symbol of intimate relation, as in v. 18 where the city is said to be called by God's name, i.e., to be a city especially close to the heart of the divine, or in v. 19 where it is said that God's people are called by His name, i.e., they are a people whose destiny and welfare are of particular concern to the divine because His name is so intimately associated with theirs. (c) The Lord's prayer opens with the invocation of the name of God ("Our father") and its first petition calls for the consecration of the divine name ("hallowed be Thy name," literally "let Thy name be sanctified").

(B) In prayer the petitioner surrenders the quest for his

or her own name (power and status) in favor of the Divine Name. (1) True prayer surrenders claims of individual and corporate achievement as grounds for being heard, and proffers instead the grounds of the divine righteousness and mercy (vv. 18, 19). (2) For those who have established credit and a known reputation for stability and reliability, a name in our society conveys status and carries with it very definite power. (3) The petitioner in prayer who invokes the name of God will not seek to rely upon his own name (reputation, status, and power) but rather upon the name of God (i.e., he will seek to hold uppermost his standing in God's sight and the power which comes from relying on God's strength and name rather than on his own).

(C) In prayer it is wisest to conclude with thoughts of the Name (i.e., power, strength, and glorious reputation) of God. (1) The prayer in Daniel we have been considering so ends. (2) The Lord's Prayer so ends ("for Thine is the kingdom and the power and the glory"). (3) Christian prayer is offered up "in the name of Jesus Christ our Lord." The meaning of this is clearly several fold: (a) by virtue of the name and status which Jesus the Christ holds in your sight, answer us; (b) by the power which Jesus the Christ confers to those who invoke His name, we offer up this prayer; (c) after the example of the One who though highly exalted humbled Himself (Phil 2:5–11), so we pray "in His name," i.e., following, insofar as we can, His model of humility and acknowledging His Lordship; (d) surrendering our claims to status on other grounds, we cast ourselves on the divine mercy manifested in Jesus the Christ; (e) thus renouncing other claims and sources of authority we not only pray in the name of Jesus but seek to rediscover the power which He gives to those who follow His path of self-giving and love. (4) By so focussing in conclusion on the majesty and strength and grace of God, the petitioner is fittingly reminded of the great resources available to him by the same majestic, omnipotent and gracious God. (5) A surprise feature in the prayer of Daniel comes at the conclusion (vv. 20–23): Gabriel, the divine messenger assures Daniel that he is "greatly beloved" and has come to bestow upon him (Daniel) wisdom and understanding. (6) May the Almighty grant to you in response to your prayers wisdom and understanding to know you also are dearly beloved.

# Heavenly Vision—
# Earthly Strength
## (Daniel 10:1— 12:13)

### Responses to Holiness (10:1–21)

Chapter ten is a parable of how confrontations with the divine have affected humanity down through the centuries: they may leave one drained and enervated (see vv. 2, 9, 10–17); on the other hand, they may invigorate and strengthen (see vv. 18–19). This chapter also illustrates well how the heavenly visions of human beings are at least in part affected by prior experiences. The visions of the angel in vv. 2–9 focus on its priestly garb ("clothed in linen," "girded with gold"). In this feature of the heavenly vision the reader is led to see but another instance of the extent to which the author of the second stage of the book was intensely interested in the temple, its sacrifices, and its personnel.

Of all the chapters in the book, chapter ten above all illustrates how the Israelites had come to believe that earthly events were affected by heavenly battles. The angel with whom Daniel converses—evidently Gabriel—relates to him how he will return to fight the prince of Persia, with Michael, the prince, at his side. Apocalyptic thus not only includes a revelation of future events but of heavenly events hidden from ordinary human sight. For a suggested sermon on Michael, the guardian angel of Israel, see below under 12:1–4. A suitable sermon on chapter ten might be entitled "Responses to Holiness."

(A) Experiences of encounter and confrontation with the Holy God invariably leave a human being with a sense of fear, trembling, awe, and veneration. (1) According to Rudolf Otto's classic study, *The Idea of the Holy*, a confrontation with the Holy leaves an individual with a clear sense of *mysterium tremendum et fascinans*, i.e., mystery, fear, and fascination. (2) In the Bible, Moses so responds before the bush which is seen to be burning and is not consumed (Exod 3:1–12). (3) Isaiah the prophet responds in a similar fashion before his vision of the holiness of God (Isa 6). (4) So it is with Daniel in chapter 10.

(B) Closer analysis of the passages which deal with the holiness and majesty of God show that a part of the typical responses is not only a sense of weakness and trembling but also a sense of uncleanness and need for purification and strength. (1) This is especially true with Isaiah's vision and to a lesser extent of Moses'. (2) In Hab 3 and Dan 10, however, there is no focussing upon the divine holiness, human awareness and uncleanness, or need for cleansing in the confrontation with the divine, but rather upon the heavenly splendor and upon human weakness and need for strengthening. (3) For Daniel out of the encounter came a touch of the divine (v. 18), an exhortation not to fear but to be strong and of good courage (v. 19) and an acknowledgment that he had been strengthened and was ready for a further word from God (v. 19). (4) The Scripture lesson thus furnishes a parable of what may come from a session of prayer, namely, the impartation of divine strength to human weakness (see also 1 Cor 1:26–31).

## History Unfolded As Prophecy/Seeing Through a Glass Darkly/The Abomination That Makes Desolate (11:1–45)

One of the recurring features in apocalyptic literature is what is known as the *vaticinium post eventum* or, literally, "prophecy after the event," that is, history which is known is told as if it were a prediction because the teller is placed back in ancient times. In chapter eleven the following are "foretold": the rise of Alexander the Great (v. 3); his demise and the division of his realm into four kingdoms (v. 4); the flourishing of the Greco-Egyptians (Ptolemies) (vv. 5–14) including the famous battle of Raphia (217 BC) in which the Greco-Egyptians were victorious (vv. 11–12) and the Battle of Paneas (198 BC) in which power over Palestine shifted from the Greco-Egyptian "kings of the South" to the Greco-Syrian "kings of the North" (Seleucids) (vv. 15–17) under Antiochus III. Here also is recorded the fateful defeat of Antiochus III at the Battle of Magnesia in Asia Minor at the hands of the Romans (190 BC; vv. 18–19).

As events get closer to, and reach, the reign of Antiochus IV Epiphanes, the Seleucid king against whom the Maccabeans revolted, the details of chapter 11 become even more precise. Verse 20 describes how the predecessor of Antiochus

sent "an exacter of tribute through the glory of the kingdom," i.e., to Jerusalem, a fact known from 2 Maccabees 4 to
correspond to the sending of Heliodorus to Jerusalem by the
king, Seleucus IV. Verses 21–39 deal with the deeds of Antiochus IV. He is called "contemptible" (v. 21) and among his
nefarious acts are included a profanation of the temple and
taking away the continual burnt offerings (v. 31) and setting
up instead "the abomination that makes desolate" (v. 31; see
1 Maccabees 1:51–63). The latter act is referred to in 9:27 and
12:11, i.e., the erection of an altar to Zeus Olympios instead
of one of "the gods of his fathers," i.e., Apollo. At Antioch,
capital city of the Greco-Syrians, Antiochus built a magnificent temple honoring Zeus. This prophecy thus fits so well
what is known of Antiochus IV Epiphanes in the years
175–167 BC, it is, in the judgment of most scholars, virtually
certain that we are dealing in 11:1–39 with a *vaticinium post
eventum*, a literary device employed in the ancient Near East
hundreds of years before the time of Daniel. Verses 40–45,
however, except for the prediction of the death of Antiochus
IV (v. 45), do not correspond to the known events during his
reign and thus constitute, including the prediction of his
death, a genuine (and not simply literary) prophecy attached
by our author to his historical survey. These verses in which
the author envisions the future bear the imprint of his consciousness of the days of monarchy after the glories of David
and Solomon when "Edom, Moab and the main part of the
Ammonites" were lost to the realm. The prophecy also re-
flects an unmistakable yearning to be rid of the wars between the Greco-Syrians and the Greco-Egyptians which had
plagued his lifetime because now at last the two realms
would be brought under one ruler. At least two sermons from
these verses suggest themselves. The first might be entitled,
"Seeing Through a Glass Darkly." It could be developed
along the following lines.

(A) The telling of history may be done in a variety of
ways. (1) One may focus upon technological advances,
mechanical inventions, farming techniques, and scientific expertise, such as Daniel Boorstin does in his series "The
Americans." (2) Or, one may focus upon economic factors,
trade, commerce, business developments, such as Charles
Beard does in his historical study of America. (3) Or, one may
focus on the lives of great persons and their achievements

such as Sirach, a writer of the second century BC, does in the book of Ecclesiasticus, chapters 44–50. (4) Or, one may tell history referring to none of the main actors by name but simply describing main personages and events in descriptive, yet indirect, terms, such as is done by the Greek-speaking and Alexandrian author of the Wisdom of Solomon, chapters 10–11. (5) Or, one may tell of historical events in symbolic terms such as is done in Dan 2, 7, and 8. (6) Or, one may tell of historical events by assuming the name of an ancient notary or sage, and then tell history *as if it were prophecy.* (a) Such is the method of the author of Dan 11. (b) It is a device used already in the ancient Near East in Egypt as far back as 2000 BC in the Admonitions of Ipuwer.

(B) The biblical-historical consciousness is varied but has several recurring features. (1) From Gen 1 to the exodus and occupation of the promised land in Joshua, the Bible sees that God has a purpose. History is not accidental but directed toward goals of freedom, growth, and development—spiritually as well as materially. (2) The events told in vv. 1–39 were historical events which came to pass. (3) Insofar as we know the events of vv. 40–45 did not. (a) The king of the north, the Greco-Syrian ruler Antiochus IV did not conquer Egypt and restore a single rule over all the Eastern Mediterranean seaboard. (b) And yet even this unfulfilled biblical prophecy is eloquent testimony of the biblical hope and faith that the wranglings and strife and bloodshed of history will one day be put to an end, that God who is sovereign over all, will effect it either directly or through his intermediary agencies. (4) We, like the author of Daniel, may see historical and future events darkly and yet we are summoned by this author to hope, and to strive, for a more peaceful future.

A second sermon on these verses might focus upon verse 31 and be entitled "The Abomination That Makes Desolate." The sermon might adopt the kind of development suggested above for 7:13–18 and seek to let the third part of the sermon (applicable to the present) emerge in the light of the first two parts (Old Testament and New Testament Message).

For a suggested introduction, see the sermon on 7:13–18. The main contours of this sermon might look like the following.

(A) *Old Testament Message.* The "abomination that makes desolate" referred to in 9:27, 11:31 and 12:11 was probably the erection of an altar to Zeus Olympios at the site of the temple, the offering of sacrifices of swine (a doubly offensive act to the pious worshipers of God in Jerusalem in the pre-Christian era), and the elimination of regular burnt offerings. Regular sacrificial worship was thus interrupted (see 1 Maccabees 1:51–63).

(B) *New Testament Message*. This same passage in Daniel became the core of a sermon preached by Jesus and later expanded after the Romans conquered Jerusalem in AD 70. The Roman desecration was reminiscent of the impiety of Antiochus IV Epiphanes who at the time of the last stage in the book of Daniel, also desecrated the temple (see Mark 13, esp. v. 14 and commentaries).

(C) *Present Day Application*. (1) During the War of Liberation in 1947–48 the Hurvah Synagogue in the Old City of Jerusalem was burned down. It may be doubted that this event should be viewed as the twentieth-century counterpart of Dan 11:31 and Mark 13:14. (2) Some conservative groups hold that the temple must be rebuilt (and then be desecrated again) before the "end" will come. (3) Such predictions may be born of a deep faith, and yet they reveal a sectarian literalism and reading of past scriptural patterns as signposts for an unfolding future. (4) The "abomination which makes desolate" which we should fear in this country in our day is that religion which (a) does away with all stress on sacrifice (self-giving), (b) so greatly exalts its leaders that they aspire to and claim the kind of adulation that the Greco-Syrians and Roman kings and emperors did, and (c) would call for an end to regular worship in favor of more spectacular public displays. (5) Perhaps it is best not to attempt to identify too closely the "abomination that makes desolate" as appropriate for someone else or some other persons who advocate programs different from the ones we favor. (6) From the theistic and Christian perspective the thing above all that "makes desolate" would be that power or force which would lead us to lose our sense of God, His power, presence and love. (7) The "abomination" may be within ourselves—the lust for power, self-importance, adulation, and the rejection of any religion that calls for steady, plodding pursuit of a way of self-sacrifice.

## Beyond Daniel 12

The Greek version of the book of Daniel which circulated in the period of the early church included a long prayer of the three children in chapter 3 and two extra chapters. These portions are usually printed separately in the writings called by Protestants The Apocrypha and as vv. 24–88 in chapter 3 and as chapters 13 and 14 in Roman Catholic translations. These additions attest to the continued popularity of the original book of Daniel. They are well-worth reading and will furnish the preacher with illustrative material on prayer, sexual ethics, idolatry, and the solving of mysteries.

Chapter 12 brings the canonical book to a dramatic climax with its teaching of the resurrection (v. 3) and then returns to an inconclusive interrogation of heavenly mediators with respect to precise calendars of the endtime (vv. 5–13). It is as if the apocalyptic writer himself sought also to dramatize how uncertain speculation on the endtime is—even for heavenly agents. Three different answers are given: $3^{1}/_{2}$ years (equals 1278 days, v. 7); 1290 days (v. 11); and 1335 days (v. 12). A sermon on predictions, including those of vv. 6–7 and 11–12, was suggested above under 8:13–19.

In terms of the movement of the book, one may proceed from chapter ten directly to chapter twelve. Chapter ten concludes with a mention of Michael and of names inscribed in the book of truth; chapter twelve opens with a mention of Michael and of people whose names are found written in the book. It almost appears as if the great historical survey and prediction in chapter eleven were an afterthought which the author or editor decided to sandwich in just before his dramatic finale.

The opening verses in chapter 12 are exceedingly rich in homiletical material. Six different sermons could be developed from them.

## Michael: Guardian of the Nation (12:1)

Michael, whose name means "Who is like God is?", is the guardian angel of the nation Israel. What vision and principles should guide a nation? Is there a difference between patriotism and nationalism? The following thoughts for a sermon on the nation have important implications for peacemaking because rampant nationalism unchecked and untamed by the principles of the biblical faith will lead inexorably to war. For additional thoughts on the nation and national responsibility, see above "National Destiny and Divine Providence" under 4:4–18. For additional thoughts on angels, see above "Outlaw Angels?" under 4:19–27. Alternative titles for this sermon on 12:1–3 might be: "What Vision for the Nation?" or "Patriotism Is Not Nationalism." The shape the sermon takes might be as follows.

(A) What guides a nation? (1) For the author of Daniel each nation had a guardian prince or angel (see also 10:20–21). This conception grew up in Israel in the post-exilic era but already had begun to develop before (see Ps 82 and Deut 32:8). (2) A modern writer (Eugen Rosenstock-Huessy) suggested that every great nation must have an ideal, a purpose, a goal larger than itself in order for its people to thrive. (a) For France it was: to be the cultural center of Europe; (b) for Britain it was: to be the one who brings peace on the seas of the world; (c) for Soviet Russia it was: to be a model for the world of how to end the economic tyranny described by Karl Marx; (d) for the United States it was: to be a model for the world of democracy and freedom. (3) A divinely appointed protector watches over us, but there is also an internal requirement. Rosenstock-Huessy was in a sense but giving expression to the biblical insight: "Where there is no vision the people perish" (Prov 29:18: KJV).

(B) What vision does this nation have? (1) It includes bringing deliverance to the oppressed. ("Give me your tired, your poor, / Your huddled masses yearning to breathe free, / The wretched refuse of your teeming shore. / Send these, the homeless, tempest-tost to me, / I lift my lamp beside the golden door": from the poem by Emma Lazarus, engraved on a tablet on the pedestal of the Statue of Liberty.) (2) It includes pursuing policies of justice. ("Then conquer we must, when our cause it is just, / And this be our motto: 'In God is our trust' ": from the Star Spangled Banner, fourth stanza.) (3) Many also believe it includes the pursuit of policies worthy of a good and compassionate God—policies which would merit recognition in the heavenly ledgers (12:1).

(C) Out of the biblical tradition we may affirm that Michael protects our nation—and also the good book holds out that a special award awaits the wise and those who turn many to righteousness. (1) The latter teaching seems to contradict the main Christian teaching that not because of any human wisdom, merit, or righteousness will ultimate salvation be attained, but only on the ground of the merits of Christ the Savior. And yet, Jesus who became our wisdom (1 Cor 1:30) surely also taught that wisdom was a virtue to be pursued (Matt 10:16) and bringing righteousness to others a worthy goal

(Matt 5:6, 10, 20; see Matt 23:23). (2) The goals of wisdom and righteousness are worthy therefore for a nation to consider even though we may no longer affirm our ultimate and final salvation will rest in them. (3) The *wise* are the ones who are sufficiently self-reliant so they do not fear for themselves; so that they may be generous, thoughtful of the needs not only of themselves but others, and skillful in discerning ways to bring self help and dignity to others. (4) Those who turn many to righteousness: (a) A part of the message of the Christian Gospel is that those who have turned to God in Christ with faith receive in return an acceptance with God and are counted as righteous. (b) Thus freed from the necessity to prove and establish our own righteousness before God—an impossible task in any event—we may turn to bring justice to others. (c) To turn others to righteousness will also include: making it desirable for others to pursue justice and to turn to God in faith not to prove themselves but to accept gratefully the mantle of righteousness He graciously bestows. (5) Patriotism, but not nationalism, may be a proper guideline for conduct and an appropriate vision to nurture. (a) A clear distinction must be made between: (i) *patriotism* (the love of one's country from within the perspective that God is parent to all countries and persons and races and nations) and may be contrasted with (ii) *nationalism* (the elevation of one's own nation so that one gives to it an uncritical and unswerving allegiance irrespective of matters of morality and justice). (b) The one form of allegiance to one's country may be affirmed by every theist, but the other is idolatrous, self-defeating and, in the end, a great disloyalty. (i) An uncritical support of country could lead to endorsement of policies which the theist is convinced on the grounds of Scripture and reason would call forth the divine judgment. (ii) The Scripture makes plain that all forms of idolatry—even idolizing one's nation—will call forth divine wrath. (iii) Patriotism will hold high the goal of seeking to bring righteousness and justice to many both within the nation and within the family of nations. (iv) An idolatrous nationalism may too easily surrender the goal of seeking justice for all.

## Resurrection (12:2)

Verse 2 is one of the few passages in the Old Testament where a belief in the resurrection of the dead is clearly articulated. Several sermons on this verse might be developed.

The first one might bear the simple title "I Believe in the Resurrection of the Dead." It could take the following shape.

(A) In Old Testament times belief in the resurrection was a late development. (1) Dan 12:1–3 is, together with Isa 26:19, one of the clearest testimonies in the Old Testament to a belief in the resurrection. (2) The idea of resurrection was well known in the ancient Near East from ancient Egypt and Canaan. (3) It did not gain acceptance in Israel until late, partly because of a strong belief in the solidarity of the generations. (If one who did wrong was not punished, one of his or her family or subsequent offspring would be: see Sirach 41:5–7. Pressure was thus removed from Israel to explain apparent injustices on the grounds of the aforementioned teaching.) (4) Belief in the resurrection was present in Judaism before the rise of Christianity. (It is expressed most clearly in the second of the Eighteen Benedictions, Shemoneh Esreh, which comes from the liturgy of the synagogue at the time of Jesus: "Thou art mighty forever, / Thou sustainest the living / And givest life to the dead. / Blessed art Thou, O Lord, who makest the dead to live.") (5) The Pharisees accepted belief in the resurrection of the dead whereas the Sadducees did not. (6) There was a heated contemporary debate between two eminent Roman Catholic scholars on the extent to which the biblical Psalms teach a resurrection. (Mitchell Dahood, S. J., in the Anchor Bible on the *Psalms* argued for its presence; Bruce Vawter, C. M., argued against it.)

(B) Belief in the two-fold resurrection found in Daniel— some to life and some to shame—is taken over in the New Testament. (1) Jesus teaches it (Matt 25:14–46). (2) St. Paul teaches it (1 Cor 15). (3) It is found elsewhere in the New Testament (Rev 7; 20:11–15).

(C) Belief in the resurrection in the New Testament is based not on an abstract principle but on the experience of encounters with the living Lord. (1) Resurrection of the body should be distinguished on the one hand from immortality of the soul (a belief found in ca. 50 BC in the Hellenized Jewish work in the Apocrypha, the Wisdom of Solomon 3:1–4) and from re-vivification and resuscitation (Lazarus raised was to die again: John 11). (2) Belief in the resurrection of Jesus was for the early Christians based upon their experiences with Him as living and present (Matt 28; Mark 16; Luke 24; John 20; 1 Cor 15). (3) Though no longer physically present, Jesus is present still with the community of the faithful at prayer, celebration of the Eucharist, and "at the right hand of the Father" to intercede in their behalf (Luke 24; John 14, 17; Heb 4:14–16; Rev 5).

A sermon on "The Biblical Doctrine of the Resurrection" might be developed as follows.

(A) For much of the Old Testament period a physical resurrection is denied even though it may be yearned for, hinted at, or metaphorically expressed. (1) The book of Job and the Psalms may be taken as typical. (a) At one point the author of Job seems to express confidence he will see God after death and be vindicated by his Redeemer (Job 19:25–26); at another he denies outright such a belief (Job 14:7–13). (The very denial, of course, makes plain that the thought has been entertained.) (b) In Ps 37 the psalmist expresses such confidence in God's protective power some exegetes have argued it was inconceivable to the psalmist that God would abandon the faithful in death. (c) Ps 139 expresses confidence that even in Sheol one will not find a place where God's spirit cannot descend. (d) On the other hand, the psalmists seem to regard Sheol as a place in which the believer will be somehow separated from God (Pss 6 and 49). (2) In both the Isaiah Apocalypse (Isa 24–27) and in Isaiah of Babylon the prophets of Isaiah's school reveal intimations of a resurrection and life after the grave (Isa 25:8; 53:10–12). (3) In Hosea and in Ezekiel the prophets speak metaphorically, if not literally, of a resurrection (Hos 6:1–3; Ezek 37). (4) The coals of belief in the resurrection were thus already glowing before they burst into the flame of explicit belief in Isa 26:19 and Dan 12:1–3.

(B) In the latter part of the Old Testament and intertestamental period, belief in the resurrection from the dead became accepted. (1) Although the graves at Qumran were oriented to the north, thus suggesting a belief in the resurrection among the Covenanters who produced the Dead Sea Scrolls, there is no explicit and unambiguous evidence of such a belief among them. (2) In the stirring book of 2 Maccabees, however, written after the horrors of severe persecution a belief in the resurrection is expressed in moving terms on the lips of a mother who has seen her seven sons put to painful and tortuous deaths:

I do not know how you came into existence in my
womb; it was not I who gave you the breath of life, nor was
it I who set in order the elements of which each of you is
composed. Therefore, since it is the Creator of the universe
who shapes each person's beginning, as He brings about the
origin of everything, He, in His mercy will give you back
both breath and life, because you now disregard yourselves
for the sake of His law.

(2 Maccabees 7:22–23)

(3) The belief is also attested in the synagogue prayer the
Shemoneh Esreh (see in the above sermon outline, A. 4).

(C) Because of their experience with the Risen Lord as
present, a resurrection for all became a deep conviction and
hope among the disciples, writers of the Gospels, and early
Christians. (1) Different modern scholars and thinkers have
sought to explain the resurrection of Jesus. (a) Dorothy
Sayers, the medieval scholar, writer of mysteries and author
of the radio play "Man Born To Be King," suggests we think in
terms of the atoms in Jesus' body re-assembling outside the
tomb. (b) The famous preacher Leslie Weatherhead suggests
we think in terms of physics—of paraffin or wax passing from
a solid to a liquid to a gaseous state. (This explanation I find
less than helpful.) (c) C. S. Lewis, the author and famous
Christian apologete, suggests we think that with the coming
of Jesus the laws of the New Age have begun to come into
effect. (d) John Knox, the renowned New Testament scholar,
urged that the resurrection of the body of Jesus should not be
separated from the descent of the Spirit; the two should be
seen as but two aspects of the same reality. (e) No matter
what explanation is offered, there can be no denying the
widespread experience among the disciples, Gospel writers,
and early Christians of Jesus alive and in their midst. (2) For
the author of the Gospel of Luke, Jesus manifested Himself at
first *incognito* but then at the sharing and breaking of the
bread (Luke 24). (3) For St. Paul the self-manifestation of
Jesus was the turning point of his life in which he recognized
he was but the last of a long line of witnesses (Gal 1:11–17; 1
Cor 15:1–11; see also Acts 9:1–19; 22:4–16; 26:9–18). (4) The
Christian Church today lives because the same Risen Lord is
experienced as present among the company of His fellowship
when it shares, breaks the bread at the Eucharist and seeks
to minister in His name to a broken world.

Preaching on the resurrection may also afford the minister with an opportunity to enter into some solid theological and doctrinal reasoning. One such sermon, "Hope, Reason and the Resurrection," might be shaped as follows.

(A) Hope in relation to faith and love. (1)—(4) (See sections C. 1—4 of the sermon on "Prediction and Hope" on 8:13–19.) (5) There is thus much promise and importance to hope. Yet, as the New Testament says with respect to the resurrection, "If in this life we who are in Christ have only hope, we are of all persons most to be pitied" (1 Cor 15:19—RSV, with "men" translated as "persons"). (6) This means that hope of itself would be rather sad if indeed the resurrection of Jesus did not take place. (7) Accordingly, Christian hope will be accompanied by faith (trust in God) that the resurrection did take place.

(B) But how reasonable is the faith that the Crucified Christ has been raised and is present still? (1) Not at all. It defies logic and ordinary experience. (2) Perhaps we cannot explain altogether satisfactorily *how* the resurrection of Jesus took place. (See above, previous sermon, section C. 1.) (3) And yet the extraordinary experience of the disciples, early Christians, and writers of the Gospels was that Jesus was indeed present still in their midst in power and in the spirit. (4) And, it continues to be our extraordinary experience.

(C) How reasonable is the hope of a future resurrection for us all: some to life, but some to shame? (1) It is crude so to assert and theologically shaky. (a) Would not a resurrection to shame constitute an admission of defeat by God if the shame were everlasting? (b) Can this particular Scripture then be the last word? (c) Are there not other affirmations elsewhere in the Bible that in the end all things will be reconciled to God and united to Him in Christ? (i) Ephesians 1:9–10 sets forth a grand scheme of God to unite all things, in heaven and in earth, through Christ. (ii) 1 Peter 3:13—4:6 addresses this question head on: there will be no final defeat of God's benevolent purposes because Christ descended into hell to preach to even the dead that they also might live to God. (iii) Both of these passages indicate that the issue of the ultimate fate of the unrighteous has been deeply reflected upon, and the conclusion drawn that an eternal damnation cannot be easily affirmed. (2) Expectation of a resurrection to everlasting shame would not seem to be reasonable for it would seem to acknowledge a limitation to God's sovereign power to save. (a) And yet: how just would God be if there were no punishment of human cruelties, torture, and other reprehensible or inhumane conduct? (b) That there would be no form of divine judgment or punishment on grave human cruelties and injustices is unthinkable. To affirm such would be the same as affirming that God is unjust and that there is no ultimate justice in God's order. (3) Reason and Scripture thus lead us to conclude that we may hope for a redressing of human wrongs, that fidelity in this life will be rewarded, that there will be some form of judgment, shame or punishment for human wrong-doing, but that ultimately in God's good time and graces His mercy will prevail over His wrath. (4) If the hope for a resurrection to everlasting life were dependent primarily on our human conduct and performance, it would not be a reasonable hope. (a) For who is there among us whose goodness and self-giving is such that he or she could count on everlasting favor as a certainty? (b) The resurrection hope, however, is based not upon our own righteousness but upon the goodness and mercy of God. (5) The resurrection hope is thus both reasonable and sound because based upon reflections on the nature of God's mercy, His power, His sovereign design for the ultimate salvation of all and the resurrection of Jesus as evidenced by His presence even among us as the Risen Lord.

## Like the Stars/Those Who Turn Many to Righteousness (12:3)

The third verse in chapter twelve is particularly pregnant and susceptible to exposition. A sermon "Like the Stars" could contain three parts: (1) The Wise: (2) Will Shine: (3) Like the Stars. The first section could explore the meaning of wisdom from the biblical perspective (see above under v. 1); the second could point out how not only in the after life, but in this life it is so that the skilled have been privileged (and thus shine); the third section could explore the desire in this life to be stars (to excel) and the biblical promise that those who pursue the wisdom of the righteous God and His Christ will flourish not only in this life but in the world to come (on which see the previous sermon outline).

A second sermon on v. 3 might focus on the phrase "those who turn many to righteousness." There is a sense in which any minister, rabbi, or priest might define the goal of his or her ministry to be "to turn many to righteousness"—the righteousness of God, the justice of God and the righteousness which is the believer's through faith (Gen 15:6). A few ideas for the development of this theme were given above in section C. of the sermon on Michael.

## *Finis*: Many Shall Roam/A Funeral Sermon (12:4–13)

It is apparent that v. 4 brings to a close one phase of the book of Daniel. Verses 5–10 and 11–13 are postscripts. In v. 4 Daniel is told to bring his words to a conclusion, to seal the book. (For a similar sentiment upon bringing a work to a conclusion, see also Deut 4:2.) The last portion of the verse, "Many shall roam, but knowledge shall increase," provides an attractive text for a sermon on the quest for meaning and the role of education. For some ideas in developing this subject, see above under 1:1–8.

Verses 5–10 deal with angelic converse and predictions of the end: for some sermon ideas on angels, see under 4:19–27 and on predictions of the end, 8:13–19. The datum that the angel is clothed in linen (v. 7), suggests an obvious, but not always noticed, priestly role played by Gabriel (the one most likely intended here), by Michael, and by the One like a Son of Man. Verse 10 provides an ideal text for a sermon on suffering as a testing, i.e., purifying, refining, process. For further ideas on this subject, see above under 3:13–23 and 24–30.

Verses 11–13 rehearse the speculations on the length of time the sacrificial worship will be cut off and of how long the "abomination that makes desolate" will perdure. The book ends with the angelic (i) injunction to wait until the end; (ii) promise of rest; and (iii) promise of an alloted place at the end of days. This verse would serve well as an outline for a sermon at the funeral of a faithful churchman or woman.

# Bibliography

Three commentaries clearly stand at the top of my list for being readable, useful for preaching, and yet scholastically sound: Andre Lacocque's *The Book of Daniel* (Atlanta: John Knox Press, 1979), Norman W. Porteous's *Daniel* (Old Testament Library; Philadelphia: Westminster Press, 1965) and E. W. Heaton's *The Book of Daniel* (Torch Bible Commentaries; London: SCM Press, 1956). More technical yet useful are the commentaries by Louis F. Hartman and Alexander A. DiLella (Anchor Bible; Garden City, NY: Doubleday, 1978), Arthur Jeffery (IB 6; Nashville: Abingdon Press, 1956) and James A. Montgomery (ICC; New York: Charles Scribner's Sons, 1927).

From a conservative point of view Joyce G. Baldwin has written a balanced and well-referenced little commentary (Tyndale Old Testament Commentaries; Downers Grove, IL: InterVarsity Press, 1978).

Journals which have devoted single issues to "apocalyptic" are: *Journal for Theology and the Church* (1969), *Interpretation* (October 1971), *Catholic Biblical Quarterly* (July 1977) and *Semeia* 14 (1979).

The last mentioned special issue was edited by John J. Collins whose *The Apocalyptic Vision of the Book of Daniel* (Harvard Semitic Monographs 16; Missoula, MT: Scholars Press, 1977) and recent *Daniel, 1 & 2 Maccabees* (The Old Testament Message; Baltimore, MD: Michael Glazier, 1982) are well worth consulting.

The best introductions to apocalyptic are H. H. Rowley, *The Relevance of Apocalyptic* (New York: Association Press, 1963), D. S. Russell, *The Method and Message of Jewish Apocalyptic* (Philadelphia: Westminster Press, 1964), and now especially George W. Nickelsburg, *Jewish Literature Between the Bible and the Mishnah: A Historical and Literary Introduction* (Philadelphia: Fortress Press, 1981).

Apocalyptic works in translation from the intertestamental period and beyond may now be found in James H. Charlesworth (ed.) *The Old Testament Pseudepigrapha*, volume I: *Apocalyptic Literature and Testaments* (Garden City, NY: Doubleday, 1983).